SO-AVR-278

Telling a Research Story
Writing a Literature Review

CHRISTINE B. FEAK
JOHN M. SWALES

VOLUME 2 OF THE REVISED AND EXPANDED EDITION OF
English in Today's Research World

The Michigan Series in English for
Academic & Professional Purposes

Copyright © by the University of Michigan 2009
All rights reserved
Published in the United States of America
The University of Michigan Press
Manufactured in the United States of America

⊗ Printed on acid-free paper

ISBN-13: 978-0-472-03336-2

2023   2022   2021   10 9

No part of this publication may be reproduced, stored in a retrieval system, or transmitted in any form or by any means, electronic, mechanical, or otherwise, without the written permission of the publisher.

Acknowledgments

We have been helped in the writing of this small volume in the new series by a considerable number of people. First, we would like to thank all the participants in our advanced writing classes, workshops, and seminars who have provided us in recent years with evaluations and suggestions for improving our materials. In addition to the University of Michigan, we have tried out earlier versions in the United States at the University of Utah, University of Maryland at College Park, and at the Perinatology Research Branch at Wayne State University in Detroit. Further afield, we have received feedback from faculty and student workshops in Brazil, Cyprus, Japan, Spain, and Turkey. We are also very grateful to those who have been willing to allow their own texts to be used as illustrative materials, whether under their own names or anonymously.

This volume would not have been completed in such a timely manner and with so few glitches without the help of our two research assistants. First, our thanks go to Rebecca Maybaum for cataloging mounds of disorganized teaching materials and for using her corpus linguistics skills to check and modify many of our statements about research English, particularly with regard to citation and tense. Second, we owe even more to Vera Irwin, for her care and attention to the evolving manuscript, for her tracking down of permissions, for her critical insights, and for her contributions to the main volume and to the accompanying online Commentary. Rebecca has now gone off to graduate school in the United Kingdom, but we hope Vera will continue to assist us in the volumes to come.

We have been able to take advantage of the many excellent suggestions for improvement made by the two anonymous reviewers. Our EAP colleagues at the English Language Institute have continued to be as supportive as ever. We also owe a great deal to Kelly Sippell of the University of Michigan Press, who, over the years, has not only become a good friend but also a great editor in the fields of ESL and Applied Linguistics. Her continuing support for us both as authors and as editors of the EAPP series has been invaluable.

Finally, on a more personal level, John would like to express his deep appreciation to Vi Benner, who quickly came to realize that retirement for John "would just be a name," and that any hopes for improvements around the house would have to wait. (Alas, the bathroom still badly needs painting.) Chris would like to say thanks to John, who still has not grown too weary of continually hearing that something "just won't work." She would also like to express her appreciation to Glen for his support of her seemingly endless list of projects.

CBF & JMS
Ann Arbor
January 2009

Grateful acknowledgment is given to the following authors, publishers, and individuals for permission to reprint copyrighted material.

R. Biswas-Diener and E. Diener for the excerpt from "The Subjective Well-Being of the Homeless and Lessons for Happiness," *Social Indicators Research*, 76, 185–205, Copyright © 2006. Permission also granted by Springer Science and Business Media.

EURASIP Journal on Image and Video Processing for the excerpt from "Color Targets: Fiducials to Help Visually Impaired People Find their Way by Camera Phone," Article ID 96357, 13 pages, doi:10.1155/2007/96357, Copyright © 2007.

Vivian Hixon for illustrations.

Mouton de Gruyter for the excerpt from "Burnout and Humor Relationship among University Lecturers," by S. Tümkaya, *Humor: International Journal of Humor Research*, 20, 73–92, Copyright © 2007.

Sage Publications for the excerpt from "Crossover of Burnout and Engagement in Work Teams," by A.B. Bakker, H. van Emmerik, and M.C. Euwema, *Work and Occupation*, 33, 464–489, Copyright © 2006.

Sage Publications for the table reprinted from "Scholars before Researchers: On the Centrality of the Dissertation Literature Review in Research Preparation" by D. Boote and P. Beile, *Educational Researcher*, 34(6), 3–15, Copyright © 2005.

Betty Samraj for the sections from her literature review.

Ron Schwad for illustrations.

Taylor and Francis for excerpts from "The Concept of Information Overload: A Review of the Literature from Organization Science, Accounting, Marketing, MIS, and Related Disciplines" by J.M. Eppler and J. Menghis, *Information Society*, 20, 323–345, Copyright © 2004.

Every effort has been made to contact the copyright holders for permission to reprint borrowed material. We regret any oversights that may have occurred and will rectify them in future printings of this book.

Contents

General Introduction to the Volumes

John and Chris first started putting together the book that became *English in Today's Research World: A Writing Guide* (henceforth *ETRW*) in early 1998. The book was largely based on teaching materials we had been developing through the 1990s for our advanced courses in dissertation writing and writing for publication at the University of Michigan. Ten years later, that "research world" and our understanding of its texts and discourses have both changed considerably. This revised and expanded series of volumes is an attempt to respond to those changes. It also attempts to respond to reactions to *ETRW* that have come from instructors and users and that have reached us directly, or through Kelly Sippell, ESL Editor at the University of Michigan Press. One consistent feature of these comments has been that *ETRW* is somewhat unwieldy because it contains too many disparate topics. In thinking about a second edition, therefore, we have made the radical decision to break the original book into several small volumes; in addition, we offer a volume principally designed for instructors and tutors of research English and for those who wish to enter this growing field of specialization. We hope in this way that instructors or independent researcher-users can choose those volumes that are most directly relevant to their own situations at any particular time.

However, we do need to stress that many of the genres we separately deal with are inter-connected. Even if a literature review is originally conceived as a freestanding object, later it is typically reshaped as part of a research project or part of a grant application. Abstracts are always abstracts of some larger text. A conference talk may be based on a dissertation chapter and may end up as an article. Grant proposals lead to technical reports, to dissertations, and to further grant proposals. To indicate these inter-connected networks, the genre network diagram (see Figure 1) we used in *ETRW* is appropriate and even more relevant to this multivolume series.

Figure 1. Academic Genre Network

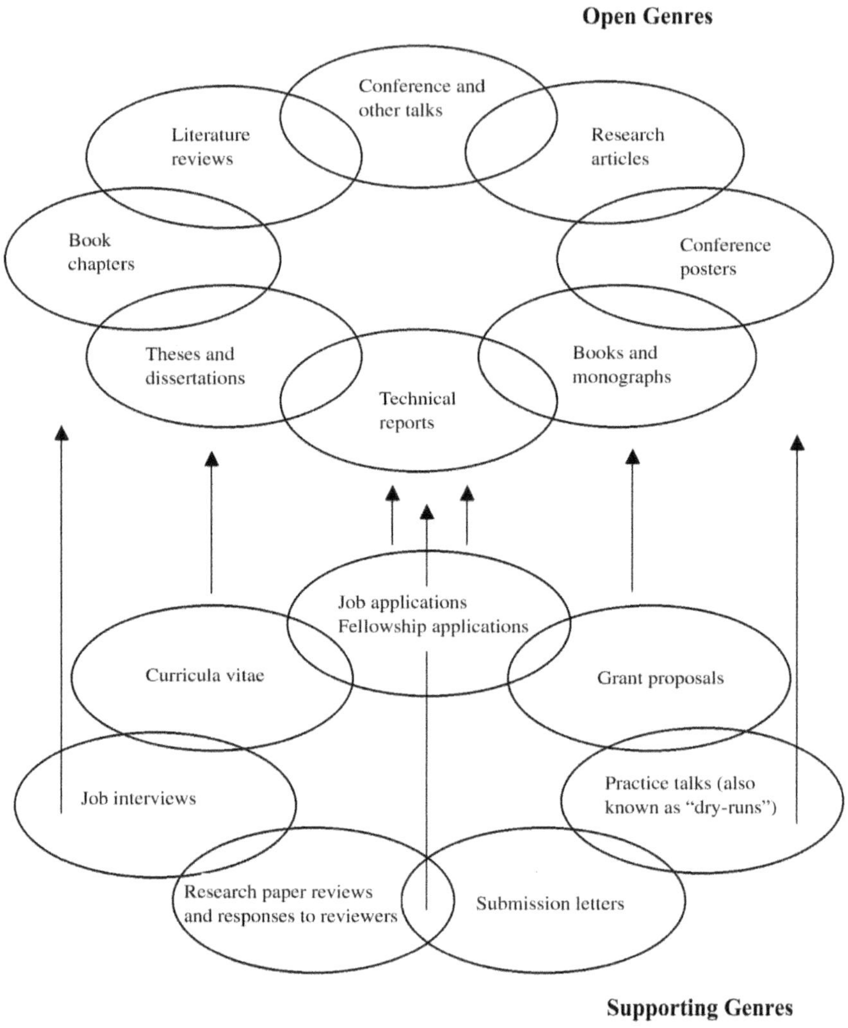

Open Genres

Conference and other talks

Literature reviews

Research articles

Book chapters

Conference posters

Theses and dissertations

Books and monographs

Technical reports

Job applications
Fellowship applications

Curricula vitae

Grant proposals

Job interviews

Practice talks (also known as "dry-runs")

Research paper reviews and responses to reviewers

Submission letters

Supporting Genres

One continuing development in the research world has been the increasing predominance of English as the vehicle for communicating research findings. Of late, this trend has been reinforced by policy decisions made by ministries of higher education, universities, and research centers that researchers and scholars will primarily receive credit for publications appearing in English-medium international journals, especially those that are included in the Institute for Scientific Information (ISI) database. Indeed, in recent years, the range of "acceptable" publication outlets has often been further narrowed to those ISI journals that have a high impact factor (in other words, those with numerous citations to articles published over the previous three years). Selected countries around the world that have apparently adopted this kind of policy include Spain, the United Kingdom, China, Brazil, Malaysia, Chile, and Sri Lanka. Competition to publish in these high-status restricted outlets is obviously increasingly tough, and the pressures on academics to publish therein are often unreasonable. A further complicating development has been the rise and spread of the so-called "article-compilation" PhD thesis or dissertation in which the candidate is expected to have an article or two published in international journals *before* graduation.

The increasing number of people in today's Anglophone research world who do not have English as their first language has meant that the traditional distinction between native speakers and non-native speakers (NNS) of English is collapsing. A number of scholars have rightly argued that we need to get rid of this discriminatory division and replace NNS with speakers of English as a lingua franca (ELF) or speakers of English as an additional language (EAL). Today, the more valid and valuable distinctions are between senior researchers and junior researchers, on the one hand, and between those who have a broad proficiency in research English across the four skills of reading, writing, listening, and speaking and those with a narrow proficiency largely restricted to the written mode, on the other.

There have also been important developments in English for Academic Purposes (EAP) and allied fields. The relevant journals have been full of articles analyzing research English, often discussing as well the pedagogical consequences of such studies. This has been particularly true of studies emanating from Spain. Indeed, the first international conference on "Publishing and presenting research internationally" was held in January 2007 at La Laguna University in the Canary Islands.

The use of corpus linguistic techniques applied to specialized electronic databases or corpora has been on the rise. The number of specialized courses and workshops has greatly expanded, partly as a way of utilizing this new knowledge but more significantly as a response to the increasing demand. Finally, information is much more widely available on the Internet about academic and research English, particularly via search engines such as Google Scholar. As is our custom, we have made much use of relevant research findings in this and our other volumes, and we—and our occasional research assistants—have undertaken discoursal studies when we found gaps in the research literature. In this process, we have also made use of a number of specialized corpora, including Ken Hyland's corpus of 240 research articles spread across eight disciplines and two others we have constructed at Michigan (one of dental research articles and the other of research articles from perinatology and ultrasound research).

In this new venture, we have revised—often extensively—material from the original textbook, deleting texts and activities that we feel do not work so well and adding new material, at least partly in response to the developments mentioned earlier in this introduction. One concept, however, that we have retained from our previous textbooks is in-depth examinations of specific language options at what seem particularly appropriate points.

As this and other volumes begin to appear, we are always interested in user response, and so we welcome comments at either or both cfeak@umich.edu or jmswales@umich.edu.

Introduction to the Literature Review Volume

It is important that we clarify at the outset what this small volume attempts and does not attempt to do. This is a volume that attempts to provide assistance during the later stages of the literature review process. In other words, it is concerned with the writing or, if you prefer, the writing up of a literature review (LR). It has not been designed to provide assistance with such preliminary explorations as finding a viable topic, using libraries or online search engines, or with note-taking or learning to use EndNote. Nor is it concerned with organizing files, managing time effectively, or structuring a research plan. To use a chess metaphor, we have focused on developing strong end games rather than strong opening moves. The topics we have stated as falling outside this book are, of course, important, but they are covered in the many websites, longer handbooks, and manuals that provide advice on how to carry out research. They also tend to be included in the increasing number of "how to" graduate courses on quantitative and qualitative research methods. Indeed, a better case can be made for providing assistance in the wider aspects of the research activity at the departmental or faculty level, rather than attempting the more general perspective adopted in this book. We should also point out that we have nothing here to say about so-called "writer's block" or other phenomena that can cause a writer to become "stuck"; we are simply not experts in this area. If a writer does get "blocked," professional assistance is usually available.

In many ways, the underlying organization of this volume is to proceed from the general to the specific or, to put it another way, to move from the macro to the micro. In this vein, we open with a number of *orientations* that are designed to raise general awareness about some of the issues that aggregate around telling the story of previous research in some area. We then address the question of how an LR might be structured and use here an extended illustrative case to underline the points we want to make. After these, we begin to zoom in on matters of language, style, and rhetoric. There is a section on explaining what you are doing (getting started) and one on using metadiscourse (writing about your text itself), both designed to help your reader see where you are going. These are followed by a fairly full discussion of various aspects of citation. Another extended case study comes next, followed by some material on paraphrasing and summarizing. The end matter of the volume contains the usual references.

In this volume, we have not offered a print *Commentary* as we did in *English in Today's Research World*, but this is available online at www.press. umich.edu/esl/compsite/ETRW/. Vera Irwin joins us as a co-author of the Commentary.

A volume of this kind raises complex issues of audience design, many of which we continue to struggle with. Instructors and tutors will likely have their own agendas and priorities, depending on whether they are assisting writers with English as a first or an additional language, which part of the world they are working in, or whether they are dealing with a group of people from the same discipline or from a number of disciplines. We therefore suggest an *à la carte* approach to the material we have presented, selecting and supplementing as seems most appropriate.

As in our other University of Michigan textbooks, we have tried to offer material from a wide range of disciplines. No one individual, whether an instructor or an individual using the volume for self-reference, is likely to be entirely happy with our selection. In this regard, we do urge users to be open-minded even when faced with research texts that look really quite distant from those they are most familiar with; often, we feel, there is something to be learned from the contrasts with those more familiar texts. After all, after we have visited a foreign country, we typically return with greater insight into our own!

We have also been thinking about genre—more specifically the type of genre in which an LR can occur. Here, we have given most space to student genres, such as LRs per se, dissertation proposals, and dissertations. However, we have by no means excluded reviewing the literature sections of research articles.

A final matter of audience design is indeed how we balance the needs of a class or a series of workshops and the needs of a graduate student or scholar using this volume on his or her own. We have tried to do this with a mix of activities; those more closed-ended tasks (the majority) can be undertaken by anybody—and, if wished, checked against the responses. In a class situation, many of the exercises are best done in pairs or groups of three.

Orientations

vsK

Why Review the Literature?

We are like dwarfs on the shoulders of giants, so that we can see more than they, and things at a greater distance, not by virtue of any sharpness of sight on our part, or any physical distinction, but because we are carried high and raised up by their giant size.[1]

—John of Salisbury, 12th century theologian and author

---

[1] A more familiar version of this thought is attributed to Isaac Newton who wrote the following in a 1676 letter to Robert Hooke: "If I have seen farther it is by standing on the shoulders of Giants."

Reference to prior literature is a defining feature of nearly all academic and research writing. Why should this be so? There are several reasons. One is to make sure that you are not simply "re-inventing the wheel"—that is, not simply replicating a research project that others have already successfully completed. American law would call this *due diligence*—in other words, doing the basic homework. A second reason is that telling a suitable story about the relevant previous work enables you to demonstrate how your current work is situated within, builds on, or departs from earlier publications. This situating is a key aspect of graduate/junior researcher positioning. A third, somewhat more subtle rationale comes from the fact that the story you have successfully told shows others that you are a member of your chosen field.

Types and Characteristics of Literature Reviews

A review of the literature can serve numerous functions, but literature reviews fall into several basic types, some of the most common of which we describe here.

Narrative Literature Review

Narrative reviews are typically found in theses, dissertations, grant and research proposals, and research articles. In such reviews, the author selects relevant past research and synthesizes it into a coherent discussion. Narrative reviews typically are somewhat broad in focus in comparison to other kinds of literature reviews, discussing methodologies, findings, and limitations in the existing body of work. Survey articles that describe the state of an area of research activity and are written by senior members of a discipline may also fall into this category. Some survey article reviews may deal with mature topics on which much has been written or with emerging topics for which sufficient literature exists to warrant an overall, evaluative analysis (Torraco, 2005). Although we will not be explicitly dealing with the writing of this type of literature review (LR) in this volume, much can be learned from seeing how the "experts" sort, describe, evaluate, and conceptualize or reconceptualize the work in your field. In fact, we will turn to sections of some expert reviews to demonstrate a few points along the way.

Systematic Literature Review

Systematic reviews follow a strict methodology in the selection of the literature that will be discussed. Thus, the criteria for including (and excluding) literature are transparent. The use of a strict protocol in choosing literature for review is thought to eliminate potential author bias. Systematic reviews are undertaken to clarify the state of existing research and the implications that should be drawn from this. Such reviews are common in the health sciences.

Meta-Analysis

Meta-analyses gather data from a number of different, independent studies that have examined the same research questions. The collective data is combined and re-analyzed using statistical techniques to gain a better understanding of a topic than is possible if only a single study is investigated. Some of these may also be systematic reviews.

Focused Literature Review

Although all literature reviews are focused, we use the term *focused literature review*, for lack of a better term, to describe literature reviews limited to a single aspect of the previous research, such as methodology. In some fields of study, students may indeed need to prepare a methodological review that examines research designs, methods, and approaches used in research on a particular issue. Such reviews describe the implications of choosing a particular methodology in terms of data collection, analysis, and interpretation. Bibliographic essays, which provide an introduction to the best resources available that discuss a topic, may also fall into this category. At our university, and we suspect at many others, bibliographic essays often are a key part of a "prelim" paper, which must be completed prior to beginning the dissertation. Such papers are typically assigned by faculty who want their students to be scholars before researchers (Boote & Beile, 2005). This distinction between scholar and researcher will be raised again at various points throughout this volume.

Task One

How would you answer these questions? (Sample answers for the tasks in the Orientations section can be found in the *Commentary* available at www.press.umich.edu/esl/compsite/ETRW/.)

1. In a thesis or dissertation in your field, should your literature review be presented in a separate chapter or is the literature reviewed as needed throughout the work? What is your own preference? And that of your advisor, supervisor, or committee?

2. How should the LR be handled in a journal article in your field? Should it be integrated into the introduction or constitute a separate section?

3. Consider these results from a study (Noguchi, 2006) suggesting that survey or review articles may fall into one of these four primary categories of focus.

    a. Historical overview (a view of some facet in the field)

    b. Current work (a look at cutting edge work in the field)

    c. Theory/Model (discussion of theories or models to resolve an issue followed by a proposal of a particular theory or model)

    d. Issue (calling attention to an issue)

    How many of the categories, if any, seem useful for the writing of your current review or review you plan to undertake?

4. Complete this chart.

	Narrative Review	Systematic Review	Meta-Analysis	Focused Review
Approximate number you have read?				
In what type of text have you read and/or found them? (dissertation, research article, other?)				
Number you have written or drafted?				

5. How well does your current (or planned) review relate to this observation by Professor Greg Myers, a well-known researcher on academic discourse?

    The successful review "draws the reader into the writer's view of what has happened, and by ordering the recent past, suggests what can be done next." (1991, p. 46)

Check Your Literature Review Knowledge

Task Two

As the next step in this Orientation section, mark with a check (✓) the items that would seem to apply to your writing situation—that is, whether you are writing something for publication or preparing the literature review for your thesis or dissertation. Do any of these seem unrealistic? If so, mark these with a double dash (- -).

Research Article	Thesis or Dissertation	
		1. The preparation of a literature review is a three-step process: finding the relevant literature, reading, and then writing up the review.
		2. Your literature review should discuss problems and/or controversies within your field.
		3. Your literature review needs to explain clearly which potential areas for inclusion have not been covered in the review and why they have been omitted.
		4. Your literature review should focus on very recent publications because they are likely the most relevant.
		5. Your literature review should be as long as possible in order to persuade your reader that you have read very widely.
		6. Your literature review should help reveal gaps in the existing body of research.
		7. Your literature review should critically evaluate each piece of work you discuss.
		8. An overall chronological ordering of the literature is a good approach.
		9. Your literature review can safely ignore work not in your immediate discipline.
		10. Your literature review can help you discover conceptual traditions and frameworks that have been used to examine problems as well as help you show how your work might contribute to a cumulative scholarly or research process.

As you consider what to include in your review and how to organize the material, it is important to keep the goals of your research in mind. This is because your literature review will need to organize the previous work in relation to your own planned or actual research. Naturally, your priorities will vary depending on the nature of your research project.

Task Three

To which of these would you give high priority (HP) and to which lower priority (LP) when planning an LR in your field?

_____ 1. Significant discoveries or findings in your research area

_____ 2. Significant and relevant concepts, models, and theories

_____ 3. Relevant methodologies in your research area

_____ 4. Gaps and needs in your field

_____ 5. The relationship between your field and other fields

_____ 6. The early history of your research area

The key surface indicator of reference to prior literature is, of course, the existence of citations on the page. While these may take many different forms (name and date, numbers, footnotes, etc.), they clearly identify a text as *academic*. As it happens, you may be surprised to know that these little citations have been seriously studied; indeed, a new field is emerging in information science called *citationology*.

There are, in fact, a surprising number of theories about the role and purpose of citations in academic writing. Eight are given in this next task to consider.

Task Four ▐▬▬▬▬▬▬▬▬▬▬▬▬▬▬▬▬▬▬▬▬▬▬▬▬

Review—and hopefully discuss—these eight theories, and then respond to the questions that follow.

1. Theory 1 is widely proposed in manuals and standard practice guides.

   Citations are used to recognize and acknowledge the intellectual property rights of authors. They are a matter of ethics and a defense against plagiarism.

2. Theory 2 also has many supporters, especially in well-established fields like the sciences.

   Citations are used to show respect to previous scholars. They recognize the history of the field by acknowledging previous achievements.

3. Theory 3 is often advocated by those working in library and information science. In our experience, this view is also popular among graduate students.

   Citations are reading guides; they point the reader to the relevant works.

The remaining theories have been proposed by individual authors.

4. Ravetz (1971):

   Citations operate as a kind of mutual reward system. Rather than pay other authors money for their contributions, writers "pay" them in citations.

5. Gilbert (1977):

   Citations are tools of persuasion; we use them to give statements greater authority.

6. Bavelas (1978):

   Citations are used to demonstrate that the author qualifies as a member of the chosen scholarly community; citations are used to demonstrate familiarity with the field.

7. Swales (1990):

> *Citations are used to create a research space for the citing author. By describing what has been done, citations point the way to what has not been done and so prepare a space for new research.*

8. White (2001):

> *Citations project what the writer perceives to be the relevant work; they establish an intellectual network.*

These more rhetorical reasons for citing the literature are interesting to discuss, and may in fact help you look at your LR endeavors as something more than just an annotated listing of related papers in your field.

1. Which of these theories contributes the *least* to your understanding of citation use?

2. Were any of these theories unfamiliar to you? Which ones?

3. Suppose you were teaching an undergraduate class and a student asked, "Why do we need to cite previous scholars and researchers?" What simple, straightforward answer would you choose?

Scholars before Researchers

The various perspectives on citations we have given may be enlightening and intellectually stimulating, as well as being quite fun! However, there are obviously some more practical considerations in the writing of a literature review.

It is generally agreed that a researcher should have some knowledge of previous work on the topic before undertaking any investigation. Underlying this belief is the notion that a review of past studies can contribute to the design of good new studies. Indeed, this is the position of Boote and Beile (2005) who argue that "a substantive, thorough, sophisticated literature review is a precondition for doing substantive, thorough, sophisticated research" (p. 3) and therefore that one must be a *scholar* before a *researcher*.[2] Others, such as Maxwell (2006), take a somewhat different perspective on

---

[2] For Boote and Beile, being a scholar means that you have an in-depth understanding of the prior work in your field; moreover, you are able to critically synthesize ideas and methods in the field, as well as understand the implications of the previous work.

the literature. While agreeing that a literature review should be the basis of any research project, Maxwell maintains that one merely needs to be familiar with the *relevant* literature to properly situate a study.

Task Five

As the previous paragraph indicates, disagreement exists as to whether a graduate student or junior scholar should be a scholar first, or can be simultaneously a scholar and a researcher. Respond to these questions.

1. Where do you stand on the issue? Do you agree with Boote and Beile or with Maxwell?

2. What might be the position of your advisor or supervisor or graduate chair (if you have one)?

3. Both Boote and Beile and Maxwell were discussing the situation in terms of educational research. Would the argument be different in a different research area? Perhaps one you know?

Typical Advisor Critiques of Literature Reviews

The final aspect of this Orientations section is a somewhat uncomfortable one because it deals with perceived weaknesses in LRs. (Indeed, for this reason, we have placed it last.)

The LR as part of a research paper, proposal, thesis, or dissertation is often thought of as a boring but necessary chore. Such LRs are often criticized but are rarely praised. After all, one rarely hears comments such as, "The most brilliant part of your thesis was the literature review!" Literature reviews in theses and dissertations also tend to be conservative in style and substance, a characteristic that may be appropriate for one's early work in the field. In fact, we know of only one really innovative literature review written by a graduate student. This occurs as Chapter 2 of Malcolm Ashmore's 1985 doctoral dissertation from the University of York (United Kingdom), subsequently published virtually unchanged by the University of Chicago Press. (See the Commentary if you would like more information. The information can be found on pages 7–8 of the Commentary.)

The LR sections of article manuscripts submitted for publication are also often targeted for criticism, sometimes in terms of missing inputs and sometimes for including far too many references. A more serious general concern is that an LR does not contribute to the argumentative shape of the introduction. In other words, the LR does not lead to the conclusion that the new research is relevant.

As you may already have experienced, advisors, supervisors, and senior scholars are often not as sympathetic as they might be to the efforts of relative newcomers to the field, such as graduate students, to construct literature reviews. "Old hands" conveniently forget that they have grown up with certain bodies of literature over many years, indeed perhaps decades. They have a firm sense of how the research has evolved over time, and they themselves have very possibly contributed to that evolution. They may have forgotten what it takes to start from the beginning, particularly in terms of what needs to be explained in the field and what does not.

Task Six

The comments of five professors and others on draft literature reviews written by graduate students or junior researchers follow. They are compilations of large numbers of observations passed on to us over the years and are not necessarily verbatim. Comment c applies mainly to the social sciences. The last specifically refers to multidisciplinary or interdisciplinary LRs. Read—and, if possible, discuss—these comments, and then respond to the questions.

a. "Your draft literature review is basically little more than a list of previous research papers in the field. While it is clearly well researched, it doesn't give me a sense of what has been more significant and less significant. It is hard to know where you stand."

b. "You have given me a chronological account, which might be fine for an encyclopedia entry or a historical background section to a textbook, but it doesn't function well as a prefacing mechanism for your own research. Although I know what your research hypothesis is, I don't see it informing your characterization of the previous literature. Somehow we need to see the relevant themes and issues more clearly."

c. "The first part of your review deals with *theory,* often invoking big names from the past. The second half deals with *practice*—in other words, more contemporary empirical findings. I don't see, at the moment, these two parts in any kind of coherent relation. I know it's hard, but . . . . "

d. "This draft literature review describes adequately each piece of relevant research but does so as a kind of anthology, piece by piece. It needs a higher pass, something that does more to evaluate and connect."

e. "Interdisciplinary reviews are hard, and I am basically sympathetic to your dilemma. However, what you have done is keep everything within its original disciplinary boundaries. To be innovative, you need to make more connections across disciplinary areas, so that we can see the new connections and relations that you will ultimately be able to establish. Good luck!"

1. Are any of the criticisms unreasonable for

   a chapter-length LR in a dissertation?

   an LR section in an RA?

   an LR written in fulfillment of a course requirement?

2. In the past, have you been the recipient of any of these five types of criticisms? Were you expecting the criticism?

3. Could any of the five criticisms apply to your current efforts?

4. Have you received criticisms of your literature reviews that we have not mentioned?

And before we leave this Orientations section, do not forget that the sheer amount of information available can be overwhelming. Consider these facts. In the biomedical field alone, for instance, it was estimated that in 1993, 3,000 new articles were published each day in the 30,000 journals of the field (Singer, Pellegrino, & Siegler, 2001). More recent estimates suggest that today this number may be closer to 6,000 (Budin, 2002).

How Can Order Be Imposed
on the Literature?

In this next section, we move on to organizing an LR. We start with a case study. Let's imagine that your dissertation research is examining the academic writing challenges of scholars for whom English is not their native language. As part of this research, you need to explore the concept of discourse community. Broadly speaking, the concept encompasses forms of communication that are created by, directed at, and used by a particular group such as scholars in a research area, bird watchers, or readers/writers of a particular entertainment magazine. See Wikipedia for more information.[1] Listed here are 27 papers dealing with the topic of discourse community (DC). What strategies could be used to impose some order on the previous work on this topic?

Porter, 1986	Olsen, 1993	Grabe and Kaplan, 1996
Cooper, 1989	Swales, 1993	Hanks, 1996
Harris, 1989	Miller, 1994	Beaufort, 1997
Swales, 1990	Schryer, 1994	Gunnarsson, 1997
Lave and Wenger, 1991	Van Nostrand, 1994	Johns, 1997
Bizzell, 1992	Berkenkotter and Huckin,	Prior, 1998
Killingsworth and	1995	Flowerdew, 2000
Gilbertson, 1992	Casanave, 1995	Pogner, 2003
Lyon, 1992	Bex, 1996	Petersen, 2007
Porter, 1992	Devitt, 1996	

What we have here is the chronological *publication* history; it is not, of course, an exact *genealogy* of the concept because many of the ideas were presented earlier at conferences and in circulated manuscripts.

One obvious approach to organizing the literature is to categorize these 27 contributions according to our understanding of the DC concept. This can be accomplished by identifying particular aspects of papers in the field. For

---

[1] http://en.wikipedia.org/wiki/Discourse_community

instance, for the topic of DC, the studies can be labeled in terms of these categories.

- their chronology in terms of publication date (as shown)
- the country of origin of the work *(provenance)*
- the discipline the writer represented (rhetoric and composition: RC; applied linguistics: AL; technical communication: TC, etc.) *(field)*
- the writer's attitude (or perspective) toward DCs: positive (+); negative (-); neutral or conflicted (=) *(perspective)*
- the type of publication: book or a shorter piece (article, etc.) *(genre)*

The results of this further categorization are presented in Table 1.

TABLE 1. Summary of the Literature on the DC Concept

Author	Date	Provenance	Field	Perspective	Genre
Porter	1986	U.S.	RC	+	Article
Cooper	1989	U.S.	RC	-	Chapter
Harris	1989	U.S.	RC	-	Article
Swales	1990	U.S.	AL	+	Book
Lave and Wenger	1991	U.S	Education	+	Book
Bizzell	1992	U.S.	RC	=	Chapter
Killingsworth and Gilbertson	1992	U.S.	TC	+	Book
Lyon	1992	U.S.	RC	-	Article
Porter	1992	U.S.	RC	+	Book
Olsen	1993	U.S.	TC	+	Article
Swales	1993	U.S.	AL	=	Article
Miller	1994	U.S.	TC	=	Article
Schryer	1994	Canada	TC	=	Article
Van Nostrand	1994	U.S.	TC	+	Chapter
Berkenkotter and Huckin	1995	U.S.	TC/AL	=	Book
Casanave	1995	Japan	AL	-	Chapter
Bex	1996	U.K.	AL	+	Book
Devitt	1996	U.S.	RC	=	Article
Grabe and Kaplan	1996	U.S.	AL	=	Book
Hanks	1996	U.S.	Anthropology	+	Book
Beaufort	1997	U.S.	RC	+	Article
Gunnarsson	1997	Sweden	Swedish studies	=	Article
Johns	1997	U.S.	AL	=	Book
Prior	1998	U.S.	RC	-	Book
Flowerdew	2000	Hong Kong	AL	+	Article
Pogner	2003	Denmark	Business	+	Article
Petersen	2007	Australia	Education	=	Article

Task Seven

The chronologically ordered matrix in Table 1 shows a five-way categorization of the relevant literature: date, provenance (country of origin), field, perspective, and genre (the kind of text). If you could choose one of the categories as your primary approach to re-organizing the literature, which would you choose? Why? (Sample answers for the tasks in this section on imposing order can be found in the *Commentary* available at www.press.umich.edu/esl/compsite/ETRW/.)

As the matrix in Table 2 indicates, we chose *perspective* as the most useful category for re-grouping the literature. This category seemed more interesting and illuminating than the others.

TABLE 2. Perspective of the Contributions

Perspective	Author	Date	Provenance	Field
-	Cooper	1989	U.S.	RC
-	Harris	1989	U.S.	RC
-	Lyon	1992	U.S.	RC
-	Casanave	1995	Japan	AL
-	Prior	1998	U.S.	RC
+	Porter	1986	U.S.	RC
+	Swales	1990	U.S.	AL
+	Lave and Wenger	1991	U.S	Education
+	Killingsworth and Gilbertson	1992	U.S.	TC
+	Porter	1992	U.S.	RC
+	Olsen	1993	U.S.	TC
+	Van Nostrand	1994	U.S.	TC
+	Bex	1996	U.K.	AL
+	Hanks	1996	U.S.	Anthropology
+	Beaufort	1997	U.S.	RC
+	Flowerdew	2000	Hong Kong	AL
+	Pogner	2003	Denmark	Business
=	Bizzell	1992	U.S.	RC
=	Swales	1993	U.S.	AL
=	Miller	1994	U.S.	TC
=	Schryer	1994	Canada	TC
=	Berkenkotter and Huckin	1995	U.S.	TC/AL
=	Devitt	1996	U.S.	RC
=	Grabe and Kaplan	1996	U.S.	AL
=	Gunnarsson	1997	Sweden	Swedish studies
=	Johns	1997	U.S.	AL
=	Petersen	2007	Australia	Education

As you can see, the guiding concept of perspective allows a kind of over-all picture to emerge; we will later see how it might be turned into a text. Thus, to get a sense of the bigger picture, we recommend this kind of matrix, or any kind of working chart, tree diagram, or table, as a useful preparatory device.

If a matrix approach does not work for you, consider using another approach known as a *mind map*—an image that depicts relationships among concepts and categories. (For further detail, check the Internet.) For our concept of discourse community, we could produce a mind map such as the one in Figure 2.

Figure 2. Discourse Community Organizational Map

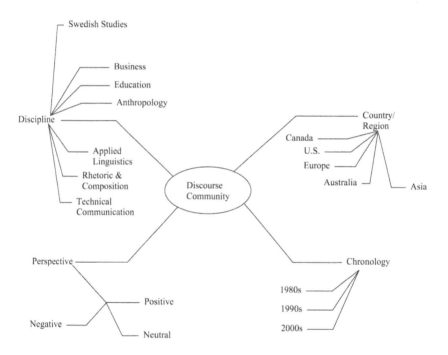

The figure can be fleshed out by adding the relevant literature that falls under each segment of the map.

Matrices and maps have four advantages, especially when we are confronted with the arduous task of putting together an LR with literature from different fields as a preface to focusing on our own work:

- They allow us to "eyeball" the literature.
- They encourage us to make connections.
- They help us avoid getting trapped in lower-level comparisons and, in so doing, we may even be able to see things that we or others have not seen before.
- Most important of all, they can point us to enough common threads so that we can, in a sense, gain a bird's-eye view or, even better, a series of bird's-eye views of what is, in its descriptive detail, highly complex material.

Task Eight

LRs in other disciplines will, of course, need to use different categories in order to impose some order on the literature. What do you think of these other possibilities? Can you add some categories of your own?

theoretical framework?   type of study?

sample size/number of cases?   computer modeling/simulation used?

practical applications stressed?

Other categories?

_____

_____

_____

_____

Which of the categorizing approaches discussed so far would work for the social sciences? Which would be appropriate for engineering and other sciences? Which would you choose for your own LR?

_____

Although organizing the literature thematically can reveal common threads as well as your grasp of the literature, this does not mean that chronology should be entirely abandoned. Within each category, you may choose to organize in order of time, especially when you are focusing on development of concepts (such as sustainable development) or technology (such as nanofiber fabrication techniques).

So, now back to the case study. Once you have a matrix or other system for grouping the literature, your next task is to decide which groups of studies to potentially include. We say potentially because you will not likely get the right combination of papers the first or second time you write your LR. Many of the papers you find and think you should include may later be discarded. Nevertheless, you need to make some decisions in order to begin.

Now that we have preliminarily grouped the relevant studies on discourse communities, we can to turn to writing a discussion of this work.

Task Nine

1. Here are some possible openings to the discussion of discourse community. Which of these do you prefer and why?

   a. According to my research, the first paper on the concept of discourse community was published in 1986.

   b. Many papers have examined the concept of discourse community.

   c. Table 2 provides a listing of 27 studies on the concept of discourse community published between 1989 and 2007.

   d. The United States has been a leading source of research on the concept of discourse community.

   e. Perspectives on the concept of discourse community vary, depending on the field of study.

   f. There seems to be little consensus as to whether the concept of discourse community is a useful one.

2. For each of these scenarios, which of the papers might you discuss first?

   a. You think that the concept of discourse community may be highly relevant for your research.

   b. You essentially agree with those studies whose perspective toward the concept is negative.

    c. You really don't know what you think yet but want (or need) to begin writing anyway.

3. One of your goals in reviewing the literature is to make a point or answer a question. For instance, one question that the studies in Table 2 can answer is this:

> *"Is the concept of discourse community useful in exploring the challenges of academic writing?"*

Do you think Questions a–d might also be answered using these studies? Pick one question, and consider how you might organize a response.

    a. Are there disciplinary differences in terms of the usefulness of the discourse community concept?

    b. How has the concept of discourse community evolved?

    c. How might the concept of discourse community contribute to our understanding of written business communications?

    d. Do bloggers constitute a discourse community?

4. Here is a draft discussing the concept of discourse community. Read it and react to the four responses to the draft that follow.

> The 27 selected studies on the concept of discourse community (DC) were published between 1989 and 2007. Most of the studies were published in the form of articles and chapters, but a small number were in the form of book-length monographs. As Table 2 shows, the great majority of the studies were undertaken in the United States, the reasons for which will be clarified later.
>
> A positive perspective toward the concept is in part dependent on the field of study. Four of the U.S. studies that question the value of the DC concept come from rhetoric and composition, while the fifth study was conducted by an applied linguist interested in empowering students whose first language is not English. On the other hand, authors in technical communications seem to like the concept of DC (Killingsworth and Gilbertson, 1992, Olsen, 1993, Van Nostrand, 1994). The applied linguists differ from the scholars in technical communication and those in rhetoric and composition.
>
> If we look closely at the different fields, it seems that rhetoric and composition is negative toward the concept of DC because it conflicts with the notion of "individual voice" of the writer, which is central to teachers of composition. However, researchers in techni-

cal communications and applied linguistics have tended to be positive toward the concept because it emphasizes the idea that writers
are part of a culture (such as business or academic) and this culture
shapes their texts.

Here are emailed comments from five professors. Which ones do you agree
with and which not? Also, briefly explain your reasons.

a. "Excellent work, my friend. You have boiled this down very well to
   three interesting and succinct paragraphs."

b. "Hi. I find this a bit wayward in its choice of detail. You deal with the
   books and chapters in Paragraph 1, but wouldn't it be better to spend
   more time on other aspects? Explanation in Paragraph 3 is interesting
   though."

c. "Thanks, I got it. But what do you mean by *The 27 selected studies*?
   Selected in what way and for what reason? Please give the criteria
   used to choose your papers first before discussing the findings."

d. "Thanks. However, on the whole I find this oddly a-chronological. In
   your account, 1986 and 2007 appear as similar, but they are in fact
   really very different. So, it's all a bit flat."

e. "Your brief LR is really short on detail, so it's not really clear what the
   studies have contributed to our understanding of DCs. I also want to
   see what you have taken away from your reading of the studies. Discuss the literature rather than gloss over it."

5. What do you think of this second version? How well does it respond to
   the criticisms in b, c, d, and e?

   Ever since the concept of discourse community (DC) first began to
   be discussed in the mid-1980s, it has had a complex and somewhat
   conflicted scholarly history. Something of this uncertainty is illustrated in Table 2, which has been structured in terms of a three-way
   category of "position." Even so, some distinct trends can be dis-
   cerned in the literature. First, much of the original work was conducted in the United States, but more recently DC-centered
   investigations have emanated from such diverse places as Hong
   Kong, Denmark, and Australia.

   Secondly, four of the five studies I identified as being "negative"
   toward the DC concept were written by scholars from the field of
   rhetoric and composition, probably because the concept conflicts
   with the notion of the "individual voice" of the writer, which is

central to many composition instructor beliefs. In fact, only three of the nine rhetoric and composition authors (Porter, 1986, 1992; Beaufort, 1997) were positively disposed toward the concept.

Thirdly, we can note much greater recognition of the value of the DC concept by those working in applied linguistics and technical communication; for example, all the technical communication authors adopted either a positive or neutral stance, and only Casanave (1995) of the applied linguistics authors was essentially negative. Researchers in these two fields have presumably largely embraced the DC concept because it stresses the idea that writers are part of a culture (whether academic or corporate) that has considerable influence on the texts that they write.

Finally, and less certainly, it would seem that in the early years, scholars tended to be either proponents or opponents of the DC concept, while more recently authors have tended to proffer more mixed conclusions. Although this last trend is quite typical of the academic world, it does leave the concept in a rather uncertain place. It remains to be seen whether it will continue to be seen as having explanatory power, or whether it will fade away.

As we suggested in the previous task, one of the potential goals of your LR should be to make a point or answer a question, ultimately guiding your reader to see the need for the research you either have undertaken or intend to undertake. To what extent does the revision do this?

Choosing Areas to Include in the Review

Given that your LR is the foundation of your research, care must be taken to tell the research story that has led you to that research. Your LR, therefore, needs to be more than a listing of previous work (Paltridge & Starfield, 2007). As Paltridge and Starfield note, through your choice to include or exclude past work, you establish a context for your work, highlighting its potential contribution to the field and extending the research story of your field in some way.

After having looked at the two write-ups of the discourse community information, we now turn our attention to another area. As with our previous example, because thesis or dissertation LRs can be rather long, we will not be able to look at a complete review on this next topic in its entirety. We will be looking at smaller parts of the LR for discussion and analysis. Before proceeding to this next task, if you have not done so already, we strongly recommend that you look at some LRs written by other students or researchers in your department.

Task Ten

Let's say you are doing research on "information overload" and student learning. You have found more than 100 papers on the topic published in journals from a variety of disciplines such as management and information systems. After reading broadly on the topic you have noticed that a large number of papers on information overload (IO) have focused primarily on its causes, symptoms, and countermeasures. However, there seems to be very little IO research distinguishing high-impact causes and countermeasures from low-impact causes and inefficient countermeasures. You have therefore decided to carry out some research to address this gap in the literature. Your advisor has suggested that you begin writing an LR to make sure that you have identified a topic that is worth pursuing—that is, the kind of preliminary review mentioned earlier.

You have created a matrix of the relevant literature and have grouped papers that address the following topics in relation to IO. Put a check next to the topics you think should be included in your review of the literature for your research focusing on distinguishing high-impact causes of IO and countermeasures from low-impact causes of IO and inefficient countermeasures.

_____ 1. IO across nations

_____ 2. Terms other than IO that refer to the same concept

_____ 3. Non-academic definitions of IO

_____ 4. Causes of IO

_____ 5. Symptoms of IO

_____ 6. A description of an individual experiencing IO

_____ 7. IO among non-human primates (such as chimpanzees and gorillas) in experimental settings

_____ 8. Something else? _____

Next, we will take a look at some important considerations in writing your LR.

Getting Started on the Literature Review

Typical LRs, like other writing you may do, have an introduction, a body, and a conclusion. In the introductory part of your LR, you may want to begin with a rather general description of your topic, highlight its importance by suggesting it is interesting, problematic, or otherwise relevant. You may then try to establish that a review of the literature is valuable in understanding important aspects of your research area. At the end of your introduction, you clarify the scope and overall organization of the review.

Writing that first paragraph of the LR can be challenging. One way to begin is by making a generalization, discussing some accepted knowledge of the field, or presenting information that is widely known. In the case of IO, you could build on the fact that the concept is well known and begin by acknowledging the everyday understanding of the term, as in the example in Task Eleven.

Task Eleven

Read this opening paragraph of a literature review on IO, and answer the questions that follow.

The Concept of Information Overload

①️ In ordinary language, the term "information overload" is often used to convey the simple notion of *receiving too much information.* ②️ Within the research community, this everyday use of the term has led to various constructs, synonyms, and related terms, such as cognitive overload (Vollmann, 1991), sensory overload (Libowski, 1975), communication overload (Meier, 1963), knowledge overload (Hunt & Newman, 1997), information fatigue syndrome (Wurman, 2001), and, more recently, information pollution (Nielsen, 2003). ③️ These constructs have been applied to a variety of situations, ranging from auditing (Simnet, 1996), to strategizing (Sparrow, 1999), business consulting (Hansen & Haas, 2001), management meetings (Grise & Gallupe, 1999/2000), and supermarket shopping (Jacoby et al., 1974; Friedmann, 1977), to name but a few overload contexts.

Source: Eppler, J. M., and Menghis, J. (2006). "The concept of information overload: A review of the literature from organization science, accounting, marketing, MIS, and related disciplines." *The Information Society 20,* 323–344.

1. How would you describe the overall organization of the paragraph?

2. What is the relationship between Sentences 1 and 2? How is connection between the two sentences established? Would the sequence be improved by the addition of a logical connector such as *however?*

3. In Sentences 2 and 3, can you identify any particular reason for the order of the different terms and situations related to IO? Would you have done something different?

4. In the first sentence, the author writes *is often used.* Why do you suppose the author chose to say *often?* Why did the author use passive voice[1] rather than active?

---

[1] Passive voice is formed by using the auxiliary verb *to be* and the past participle of a verb. The subject of the passive sentence is the recipient of the action/verb. For example, *This paper was published last year.*

5. In Sentence 1, the author uses the present tense *(is often used)*, but in Sentences 2 and 3 the author uses present perfect.[2] Why?

6. What do you think would be a good topic to follow this rather general opening? (Sample answers for the tasks in Getting Started on the Literature Review section can be found in the *Commentary* at www.press.umich.edu/esl/compsite/ETRW/.)

Describing the Selection Criteria for Literature in the Review

No doubt, during the writing of your LR you will have many questions regarding what work to include (or exclude). Despite your best effort to make the right choices, questions of inclusion may persist even into the dissertation defense stage. Consider this extract from a U.S. dissertation defense on the topic of artificial intelligence. The committee member opens the exchange with a negative comment. What is it?

Dissertation Committee Member: . . . what I'm trying to say is there's a growing literature on factoring, you know on aggregating factoring, Markov chains and you turned a blind eye to that literature.

Graduate Student: I referenced a couple of papers but then I didn't go into details of what they're doing.

Dissertation Committee Member: Why were you convinced that that was the wrong way to go?

Graduate Student: Well, for several reasons. One because they talk about aggregating states in terms of abstraction and feature extraction things like that but they don't really consider plan execution and making that real-time at all. So they don't, they don't produce part two of the plan.

---

[2] Present perfect is formed by using a form of the verb *have* and the past participle of a verb. For instance, *I have finished my literature review.*

They don't think about deadlines, so in order to think about deadlines you first have to guess at which deadlines you needed, and then you'd have to consider those as separate actions for your transition matrix.

<u>Source</u>: MICASE. Artificial Intelligence Dissertation Defense; File ID: DEF270SF061

Now look back at Task Two, Statement 3 (page 5). Would you say that the graduate student candidate is in some trouble for paying insufficient attention to the literature on factoring? Was the candidate's response adequate?

As the excerpt from the dissertation defense indicates, your LR readers may have certain expectations regarding what papers or research will be included in your review. Therefore, depending on your field of study, you may want to include some discussion of how you identified the papers for inclusion. Let's begin by looking at an excerpt from a systematic review. As described earlier on page 3, systematic reviews employ a clear methodology to select (and reject) papers for inclusion (and exclusion). Although it is unlikely that you will be required to provide such a specific accounting of your choices, it is interesting to see the thought process so clearly laid out in the text below.

Task Twelve

Read the excerpt from a systematic review of research published in the 1990s on motorcycle injury costs. This section explains the choice to include 25 studies out of a potential 200.[3] Note the range of verbs and exceptional level of detail. Answer the questions that follow.

We began the process by considering a number of articles and sources recommended by our team's senior economists and by NHTSA staff. To supplement these, we conducted searches on Medline and Transportation Research Information Service (TRIS) for articles from the medical and transportation fields, respectively, that addressed motorcycle injury costs. (Appendix D shows the search terms that were used.) We also con-

---

[3] There are some similarities here to research papers in medicine that describe the inclusion and exclusion criteria for patients in a study.

tacted researchers in other countries for suggestions of articles we might have missed in the United States. All together, we located references to nearly 200 publications from the motorcycle literature of the 1990s.

Only a few of these articles met the criteria for inclusion in this study. We dropped most articles that did not directly address the costs of motorcycle injuries, excepting a few articles that made unique contributions to the literature. We also eliminated studies that did not include human subjects, articles that did not present or review original research (e.g., documents that merely expressed the author's opinion without presenting new facts or data), and studies that were not in the English language. We eliminated more than one-third of the articles based on a cursory look at the title and abstract. We eventually narrowed the list to fewer than 80 articles that looked like they might meet our criteria, and we set about obtaining these articles. We found that most of these articles did not directly address the costs of motorcycle injuries, and we slowly further narrowed the list to the 25 studies on which this literature survey is based (see Table 3).

Source: www.nhtsa.gov/people/injury/pedbimot/motorcycle/Motorcycle_HTML/overview. html#3

1. How common are systematic reviews in your field? Do LRs in your field typically explain how the literature under review was chosen? What are the possible advantages and disadvantages of highlighting your selection criteria?

2. What do you think of the authors' decision to exclude literature not written in English? Can you think of any reasons why this could be a bad decision? Will you limit your own LR to research published in English? Why?

3. List the verbs used in association with the selection process. Can you think of any other verbs that could be used? Does this list suggest anything to you?

TABLE 3. Motorcycle Injury Publications

Authors and Year of Publication	Focus	Period of Study	Locale of Study	Sample Size	Method	Helmet Use Recorded?
Begg, Langley, & Reeder (1994)	Epidemiology	1988	New Zealand	2,623	National hospital census	No
Begg, Langley, & Reeder (1994)	Epidemiology	1978–87	New Zealand	1,175	National mortality census	No
Billheimer (1998)	Training	1977–95	California	2,351	Matched pair study	No
Braddock, Schwartz, Lapidus, Banco, & Jacobs (1992)	Epidemiology	1986–89	Connecticut	1,020	State hospital census	No
Braddock, Schwartz, Lapidus, Banco, & Jacobs (1992)	Epidemiology	1985–87	Connecticut	112	State fatality census	Yes
Bray, Szabo, Timmerman, Yen, & Madison (1985)	Cost estimates	1980–83	Sacramento, Calif.	51	Single-institution census	No
Bried, Cordasco, & Volz (1987)	Epidemiology & costs	Jul 84–Jun 85	Tucson, Arizona	71	Single-institution census	Yes
Hell & Lob (1993)		1985–90	Munich, Germany	210	Local police report census	Yes
Karlson & Quade (1994)	Head injury	1991	Wisconsin	3,184	State census—linked	Yes
Kelly, Sanson, Strange, & Orsay (1991)	Helmet-nonhelmet comparison	Apr–Oct 1988	8 Illinois hospitals	398	Hospital census	Yes
Max, Stark, & Root (1998)	Helmet law evaluation	1991–93	California	11,163	Hospital census—pre-post	No
McSwain & Belles (1990)	Helmet law evaluation	Sep 86–Dec 87	Bexar Cty, TX	99	EMS census	Yes
McSwain & Belles (1990)	Helmet law evaluation	Jun-Sep 81–82	3 LA cities	616	Linked datasets—pre-post	No
McSwain & Belles (1990)	Helmet law evaluation	1981–87	Louisiana	15,741	Fatality census	No
Miller, Levy, Spicer, & Lestina (1998, 1999)	Costs by vehicle type	1992–93	United States	ca. 1,000	Computed from national surveys	No
Muelleman, Mlinek, & Collicott (1992)	Helmet law evaluation	1988–89	2 Nebraska counties	671	Linked datasets—pre-post	Yes
Murdock & Waxman (1991)	Helmet use evaluation	45 months	Irvine, California	474	Single-institution census	Yes
NHTSA (1996, 1998)	Helmet use evaluation	1991	7 states	10,353	State census-linked	Yes
Nelson, Sklar, Skipper, & McFeeley (1992)	Helmet use & alcohol	1984–88	New Mexico	206	Fatality census	Yes

Author	Study purpose	Date	Location	Sample size	Data type	Cost by surrogate-based AIS
Newman, Tylko, & Miller (1994)	Bio-mechanical cost model	NA	NA	NA	Cost by surrogate-based AIS	NA
Offner, Rivara, & Maier (1992)	Helmet use evaluation	1985-89	Seattle, WA	425	Single-institution census	Yes
Orsay, Holden, Williams, & Lumpkin (1995)	Helmet use evaluation	Jul 91–Dec 92	Illinois	1,231	Trauma registry census	Yes
Rowland, Rivara, Salzberg, Soderberg, Maier, & Koepsell (1996)	Helmet use evaluation	1989	Wash. State	386	State census—linked	Yes
Rutledge & Stutts (1993)	Helmet use evaluation	Oct 87–Dec 90	NC's 8 trauma centers	892	Trauma registry census	Yes
Shankar, Ramzy, Soderstrom, Dischinger, & Clark (1992)	Helmet use evaluation	Jul 87–Jun 88	Maryland	1,900	State census—linked	Yes
Stutts, Rutledge, & Martell (1991)	Compare m'cycle vs. other	Oct 87–Dec 90	NC's 8 trauma centers	774	Trauma registry census—link	Yes
Tsauo, Hwang, Chiu, Hung, & Wang (1999)	Helmet use evaluation	Jul 89–Jun 94	Taipei, Taiwan	400	Random sample of head injuries	Yes
Wang, Knipling, & Blincoe (1999)	Crash risk & cost methods	1989–93	United States	NA	Computed from national surveys	No
Weiss (1992)	Helmet use evaluation	1976-77	LA, Calif.	770	Probit model of head inj severity	Yes
Weiss (1992)	Helmet use evaluation	1985	Seattle, WA	105	Single-institution census	Yes

Source: www.nhtsa.gov/people/injury/pedbimot/motorcycle/Motorcycle_HTML/overview.html#3

4. Nearly every sentence begins with *we*. If this review were written by a single author, would first person *(I)* be okay? If not, how would you rewrite the text as a single author?

5. Look at the article matrix in Table 3 that accompanied the original article. How does this compare to the matrix in Table 2? Do you see any useful ways of organizing the literature? Consider again how such a matrix might be useful to you.

The previous sample text (see pages 26–27) describing the literature included in the review came from a systematic review. Now let's look at an example of how a dissertation writer handled the discussion of what was included in her literature review. First, we provide some background. Betty Samraj was writing her dissertation in Linguistics. Her working topic was graduate student writing in interdisciplinary contexts, as represented by the university's School of Natural Resources and the Environment (SNRE). Betty organized her literature review in this manner.

Task Thirteen presents Betty's introduction to her 22-page LR.

Task Thirteen

Read the LR introduction, and answer the questions after the text. Sentence numbers have been added for ease of reference.

①In the opening chapter I have attempted to outline and motivate my study of graduate student writing in a school of natural resources and environment. ② The purpose of this chapter is to relate this study to previous scholarly attempts to describe, analyze and explain academic writing and the processes of its acquisition. ③ One purpose here is to establish what has been revealed in other academic contexts as a basis for the findings of my study. ④ Another purpose is to attempt a general critical evaluation of the research so far.

⑤ The amount of potentially relevant literature is very large and comes from various sources: composition specialists, social construction-ists, EAP/ESL (English for Academic Purposes/English as a Second Language) specialists, and discourse analysts. ⑥ For my purposes, I will concentrate on the studies in undergraduate writing tied to the writing-across-the-curriculum (WAC) movement, graduate student writing (produced both by native and non-native speakers of English) and disci-plinary rhetoric, with special attention given to interdisciplinary and environmental discourses.

Source: Samraj, 1995, p. 28.

1. The passage opens with *In the opening chapter I have attempted to . . . .* As you can see, the verb is in the present perfect. She could have written, *In the opening chapter I attempted to . . . .* What is her strategic motive for choosing the present perfect?

2. The remaining three sentences of the first paragraph open in a similar way but are written in the present tense.

   The purpose of this chapter is to relate . . .

   One purpose here is to establish . . .

   Another purpose is to attempt . . .

What is the technical name for this kind of language?

What might be the positive and negative aspects of such repetitions?

3. Consider a sentence like, *The amount of potentially relevant literature is very large.* Which of these choices might you expect to follow such a sentence?

   ; therefore, this review will be rather long.

   ; therefore, it will be divided into a number of sections.

   ; however, I will principally focus on . . .

4. Sentence 6 opens with *For my purposes, . . .* In your view does this refer back to the purposes mentioned in the first paragraph? Or does it refer forward, as in *For the purposes of the arguments that I am going to make . . .?*

5. As we have already noted, in their 2005 article, Boote and Beile (2005) maintain that, for doctoral students, "the onus [responsibility] is on doctoral candidates to convince their readers that they have thoroughly mined the existing literature and purposefully decided what to review." Does it seem that Betty will successfully bear this onus?

Doctoral candidates are novice researchers almost by definition and do not have the luxury of being assumed to know the literature. For that reason, we believe that they can demonstrate their knowledge or comfort level with the literature by clarifying how they selected the literature in their review.

Linking Sections of the Review

Another challenge in writing the review is linking different sections of the review so that the flow of information is smooth. Let's now return to the information overload literature review. In reviewing the relevant studies of IO, it seems reasonable to include sections on the causes and effects/ symptoms of this phenomenon. Let's assume you have already discussed the causes of IO and are ready to begin talking about its symptoms or effects.

Task Fourteen

Read this section from the literature review on information overload. The beginning of this excerpt consists of the last two sentences of the previous section on the causes. Answer the questions after the text.

① Having reviewed the major causes of information overload and their impact on IPC and IPR, I will now examine their effects or observable symptoms.

Symptoms of Information Overload

② One of the first researchers to examine the effects of overload was the American psychologist Stanley Milgram (1970), who analyzed signal overload for people living in large cities. ③ In his study, he identified six common reactions to the constant exposure to heavy information load, which are allocation of less time to each input, disregard of low-priority inputs, redrawing of boundaries in some social transactions to shift the burden of overload to the other party of the exchange, reduction of inputs by filtering devices, refusal of communication reception (via unlisted telephone numbers, unfriendly facial expressions, etc.), and finally creation of specialized institutions to absorb inputs that would otherwise swamp the individual (see also Weick, 1970, for this point).

④ In the organizational context, frequently described symptoms of information overload on the individual level are a general lack of perspective (Schick et al., 1990), cognitive strain and stress (Malhotra,

1982; Schick et al., 1990), a greater tolerance of error (Sparrow, 1999), lower job satisfaction (Jacoby, 1984), and the inability to use information to make a decision (Bawden, 2001)—the so-called paralysis by analysis. ⑤ Many other symptoms noted by different researchers are listed in Table 4.

⑥ The big question with regard to effects of information overload is whether and how it impacts decision accuracy, decision time, and general performance. ⑦ While research results have often been contradictory, especially among the groundbreaking studies in marketing (the inconsistencies were in part due to methodological problems; see Jacoby et al., 1974; Malhotra et al., 1982; Muller, 1984), there is wide consensus today that heavy information load can affect the performance of an individual negatively (whether measured in terms of accuracy or speed). ⑧ When information supply exceeds the information-processing capacity, a person has difficulties in identifying the relevant information (Jacoby, 1977), becomes highly selective and ignores a large amount of information (Bawden, 2001; Herbig & Kramer, 1994; Sparrow, 1999), has difficulties in identifying the relationship between details and the overall perspective (Schneider, 1987), needs more time to reach a decision (Jacoby, 1984), and finally does not reach a decision of adequate accuracy (Malhotra, 1982). ⑨ Because of these many potential negative effects, it is important to devise effective countermeasures. ⑩ These countermeasures should address not only the symptoms of information overload but also its causes. ⑪ In the next subsection I provide an overview of such mechanisms.

Source: Eppler, J. M., and Menghis, J. (2004). The concept of information overload: A review of literature from organization science, accounting, marketing, MIS, and related disciplines. *The Information Society 20*, 325–344.

1. How is the symptoms section organized?

2. What is the purpose of Sentences 1 and 11? Do you know what sentences like these are called?

3. Why do you suppose there is a fair amount of discussion of Milgram's work?

4. Very little detail is given for the majority of studies. Why? Do you think that listing studies is a good strategy for your literature review?

5. Do you think that you can or should include in your literature review a table that gives a snapshot of relevant studies?

6. What kind of evaluation is present in this section? Underline the evaluative language. How important is it for you to reveal your perspective toward the literature in your review?

7. The only scholar mentioned by first name in this section is Stanley Milgram. Because he is included as a grammatical part of the sentence, this citation is called an integral citation. (See page 45.) The remaining citations are non-integral—that is, they are not part of the structure of the sentence. What is the effect of primarily using non-integral citations?

8. As an aside, do you recognize symptoms of IO in your own busy life?

Now it's time for you to attempt a short synthesis of literature. Even if you are not in the field of biology, we think you can now make a reasonable attempt at shaping the notes given here into a reasonable review.

Task Fifteen

We want you to approach this task as if you were a junior researcher doing a study of endangered species. You are now beginning to think about the literature on butterflies. Read through these summaries of research on the butterfly Mitchell's Satyr (pronounced say-ter). Read the very short abstracts and then consider the questions and writing task after them.

State of Michigan website 2002

Mitchell's Satyr is one of the world's rarest butterflies, today found only in the northern U.S. states of Michigan and Indiana. Mitchell's Satyr is a dark, chocolate brown butterfly with eyespots and two reddish bands on its underwing. It only flies for three weeks each year, typically in the first three weeks of July. It is a federally endangered species. It needs a special kind of wetland habitat consisting of sedge fens with scattered trees.

Glassberg, J. 1993

Mitchell's Satyr was eliminated in the 1980s from its last remaining fens in the state of New Jersey because of collecting pressure by butterfly collectors.

U.S. Fish and Wildlife Service: Federal and State Endangered and Threatened Species Expenditures 2000

Mitchell's Satyr was listed as federally endangered in 1992. No endangered species can be collected without a special permit. In 1999, the federal government spent $65,000 on protecting Mitchell's Satyr and the states $22,000.

Shuey, J. A. 1997

Of slightly more than 30 known historical populations, eleven existing populations are known from southern Michigan and one from northern Indiana. While some populations have been lost through habitat loss; for others, no overt cause of extinction is obvious.

J. Szymanski, J. A. Shuey, and K. Oberhauser, 2004

Population sizes are small, and they occupy small areas of the fens. Neither males nor females fly very far. These factors make them vulnerable to disturbance.

Barton, B. 2007

After considerable research, we know that 17 populations survive in Michigan and two in Indiana (Hyde et al., 2001). Unfortunately the remaining sites are small and isolated from one another. Another problem is that it is also not fully clear which plants the butterfly larvae feed on. Immediate recovery efforts should focus on improving and enlarging existing habitats; over the longer term, possible ways of connecting some of the existing populations need to be explored.

1. What point could you argue by using the literature in these summaries? List as many points as you can.

2. Write a review of the literature in such a way that allows you to make one argument from the list you created. Make some use of each entry if possible but, of course, be selective in what you retain. Try not to use the exact words, and try to avoid quotation marks because biologists rarely use them. Decide on a suitable introductory sentence, and try to connect and link the findings, etc., in the various publications. Aim for about 200 words (the entries total about 315 words).

Metadiscourse

No doubt you need to consider your audience as you write. If you have a good sense of your audience, you can also get a sense of what kind of information you need to give your readers so that they may follow your discussion. One way that writers can help their audience to understand their text is by using metadiscourse or elements in a written text that refer to the text itself. Put simply, it is "discourse about discourse." As Williams (2007) states, metadiscourse is writing about the evolving text rather than referring to the subject matter. Metadiscourse is an important part of our everyday language, and "a major feature of the ways we communicate in a range of genres and settings" (Hyland, 1998). You have already seen examples of metadiscourse in Tasks Thirteen and Fourteen.

Metadiscoursal elements do not add propositional material (content); rather they are intended to help readers make their way through a text by revealing its organization, highlighting important parts, and evaluating, among other things. For example:

- *Part I of this review traces* the development of section 4B of the Clayton Act.
- The negative aspects of recycling plastics *will be taken up in the next section.*
- *This section examines studies of* the potential of recycled PET as a material for the clothing industry.

As you can see from these few examples, the metadiscourse phrases enable the author to intrude into his or her text (in a way to talk to the readers) in order to direct or engage the readers in some way (Crismore & Farnsworth, 1990).

One of the primary roles of metadiscourse is to reduce the cognitive load on our imagined readers. It aids communication, helps support a writer's position, and serves to build a relationship with an audience (Hyland, 1998). As such, it is not surprising that the amount and kind of metadiscourse in English is influenced by a number of factors.

1. Other things being equal, there is likely to be proportionately more metadiscourse in longer rather than shorter academic texts. After all, longer texts impose a greater memory load and are not likely to be

read in one sitting. Thus, metadiscourse is particularly associated with academic books, dissertations, and theses.

2. The type of text you are writing will influence the type of metadiscourse that you use. Expository texts require more metadiscourse than do narratives.

3. There is some variation across disciplines in terms of the type and amount of metadiscourse used (Hyland, 1998).

4. Metadiscourse is more often used to support complex rather than straightforward material. This is at least part of the reason why metadiscourse is particularly prevalent in philosophy.

5. Metadiscourse is also common in extensive spoken monologues, such as lectures and colloquia, presumably again to reduce the cognitive and memory load.

6. Metadiscourse is also common in instructional material, such as in textbooks.

7. Metadiscourse is more likely at the beginnings and ends of sections, chapters, papers, lectures, etc.

8. Attitudes regarding the value of metadiscourse vary across cultures. Some academic cultures consider extensive use of metadiscourse to be offensive to the reader (Mauranen, 1993).

Here are a few examples of metadiscourse that reveal the organization of an LR.

Future Projections

In this section, I will discuss the past and current applications of the theory.

This part will describe previous attempts to produce biofuels under supercritical conditions.

Present Orientations

For the time being, we will simply assume a market of perfect competition.

At this point, the reader may recognize that . . .

Recapitulations

The main purpose of this review has been to examine whether . . .

Thus far, this review has outlined the need for further development of vehicle-safety communication systems.

Task Sixteen

Try to determine whether the statements are intended to provide a future orientation (F), present orientation (P), or a recapitulation (R).

_____ 1. This review has four principal sections: . . . .

_____ 2. It has not been possible in this review to consider all . . . .

_____ 3. In the remainder of this review, this constant will be referred to as Q.

_____ 4. In order to see why this crisis has arisen, it is first necessary to examine . . . .

_____ 5. We can now turn to the second type of supporting evidence.

_____ 6. As the reader may have noticed in this last section, the most interesting results are those that relate to . . . .

_____ 7. Here it is important to note that this use of the term _preference_ is not identical to . . . .

_____ 8. Each of these theories will be examined in turn.

Task Seventeen

Here is a first draft of an overview of a dissertation proposal literature review written by a student in economics. As you can see, the text contains a reasonable amount of metadiscourse.

1. What stylistic criticisms might be made in regard to this overview?

This review is organized as follows. Section 2 describes the early the theoretical work. Section 3 presents more recent work on the Fiscal Policy Model. Section 3 discusses the relevant statistical and computational analyses as well as the hypothesis testing and its interpretation. Section 4 summarizes the findings and provides a brief discussion concerning the shortcomings of the methods employed.

2. What changes were made in this revision of the original?

This review is organized as follows. Section 2 describes the early theoretical concept. In Section 3, more recent work on the Fiscal Policy Model is presented. This section also discusses the relevant statistical and computational analyses as well as the hypothesis testing and its interpretation. Finally, the findings of these analyses are summarized and a brief discussion concerning the shortcomings of the methods employed is provided in Section 4.

3. At the end of your LR, you may want to consider providing a recapitulation of your work reminding your reader of what you have accomplished in your LR. How could you rewrite the overview as a retrospective summary?

Citation Patterns

When referring to prior literature you will have a number of decisions to make. Of course, a main consideration will have to do with content—what information you should extract from your source. Beyond content, however, you will need to consider whether to directly quote from your source or whether to paraphrase or summarize. You will also need to decide which studies to discuss as a group and which to discuss alone. Although these decisions may not be so easy, fortunately, the actual citation patterns that you use to refer to previous work are somewhat more straightforward. Citation patterns, as outlined in the various style guides available for each field, are limited to a few options. These options may be further limited by preferences of your chosen discipline.

Task Eighteen

Mark the citation patterns as likely (+) or unlikely (–) in your field of study. If you are not sure, place a question mark (?) next to the item.

_____ 1. direct sentence quotation

_____ 2. block quotation of 40 words or more than four lines (such quotations are indented and visually distinct from the surrounding text)

_____ 3. paraphrase (using your own original words to restate information from a source)

_____ 4. a one-sentence general summary of several sources

One study of citation patterns in journal articles from eight disciplines (Hyland, 1999) revealed some interesting disciplinary variation.

TABLE 4. Percentages for Each Citation Option According to Discipline

Discipline	Quotation	Block Quotation	Summary/ Paraphrase	Generalization	Other
Biology	0	0	72	38	
Physics	0	0	68	32	
Electrical Engineering	0	0	66	34	
Mechanical Engineering	0	0	67	33	
Medicine	0	0	61	37	2[1]
Marketing	3	2	68	27	
Education	20	1	55	20	3[2]
Applied Linguistics	8	2	67	23	
Sociology	8	5	69	18	
Philosophy	2	1	89	8	

Source: Data from Hyland, K. (1999). Academic attribution: Citation and the construction of disciplinary knowledge, *Applied Linguistics 20*, 341–367. Data for education and medicine were compiled by Vera Irwin.

[1] These were referral citations that instruct the reader to see another paper for further information on a topic. For instance, *For further detail, see Benfield (2004).*

[2] All of these were "hybrid" citations consisting of one or more short quoted phrases and original wording of the author. For example: *Universities were everywhere being pressed to consider that "education was good for business" (Howes, 1956).*

Task Nineteen

Analyze the table, and then find out more about citation patterns in your own field.

1. What percentage of citations in your field would likely involve a quotation?

2. Why do you suppose Sociology and Applied Linguistics have the highest percentage of citations in the form of quotations from previous authors' works?

3. Note the percentages for generalizations. If you had to guess, would you say the differences might reflect (a) the size of the field, (b) the shared goals of the field, or (c) some other cause?

4. Note that no quotations at all were found in any of the science and engineering research papers. Under what circumstances might one occur?

5. Do you think any of your responses would be different for a dissertation or thesis?

6. Take two research articles in your field or a section of a dissertation LR and analyze them in terms of the categories in Table 4.

Integral and Non-Integral Citations

Another important variable is whether the name(s) of the cited author(s) is a grammatical part of the citing sentence or stands outside it, either in parentheses or as represented by a number. (See style sheets in your field to see how this is done.) The former are often called *integral* citations and the latter *non-integral* ones. Integral citations tend to focus the attention more on the researcher and rather less on the research. Thus, these citations are also sometimes referred to as *author prominent,* while non-integral citations are also called *research prominent* citations. Here are some examples.

Integral (author prominent)

Muehlbach and Walsh (1995) examined the effects of caffeine administered during a night-shift and its effects on subsequent daytime sleep.

According to Jay et al. (2006), about 25 percent of the labor force in industrialized countries is involved in some form of shift-work.

Kim (2007) found that the strain rate and DIF can be misinterpreted depending on the calculations used to determine them.

Differences between exporting countries and importing countries have been extensively studied by Ikamata (2007).

Non-Integral (research prominent)

Research has illustrated that administering caffeine to sleepy individuals has several benefits. Numerous studies have reported caffeine-related reductions in both subjective sleepiness [8], [9], [10] and [11], and objective measures such as sustained reaction time (RT) [12] and driving [7] performance.

Research indicates that near to 50 percent of night-shift workers extend their normal hours of wakefulness from the average 16 to 24h on the first night-shift of their schedule (Akerstedt, 1995).

Integral citations in which the study authors are the grammatical subject of the sentence typically focus on only one or possibly two studies. (Occasionally, you may find three studies but not likely more than that.) In a passive construction, it may be possible to have perhaps as many as three studies in the *by* phrase but not likely more.

Hyland's study (1999) of journal articles also found that non-integral citations made up the majority of citations in all fields but one—Philosophy. However, in her 2006 study of reporting clauses (verb [e.g., *state, show, suggest*] + *that* clause) in dissertations from Political Science and Materials Science, Charles (2006) found a very different pattern, namely a marked preference for integral citations.

So, what might account for this difference? It is possible that Charles's narrow focus on reporting verb + *that* clause as opposed to all citations could have skewed the results. At the same time, there may very well be differences in the typical citation patterns of journal articles and dissertations, especially when we consider the unique characteristics of each.

Task Twenty

Consider the differences between a journal article and a dissertation in terms of citation style preferences. You may wish to consider such aspects as audience, overall purpose, or length. How might these differences contribute to the choice of integral or non-integral citation?

Given that integral citations generally narrowly focus on one or two studies, it is not surprising that they may predominate in an LR, where you are expected to discuss some of the previous work in some detail, rather than consolidate many studies and make general comments. (Indeed one of the problems with the text on pages 19–20 in Task Nine was that there was essentially no discussion of the individual studies. See also the second draft in Task Twenty-Five on page 66.) By focusing on individual studies you may be able to indicate your own perspective toward the literature and more easily position your research with respect to the body of existing work (Charles, 2006).

Citation Verb Tense and Aspect

As we indicated earlier, you will need to decide which verb tenses and aspects to use with your citations. This is one of those aspects of academic writing for which we can give some general guidelines that then need to be tested against exemplars of writing from your own field. You may find that the guidelines we provide work rather well for your field. In other cases, you may find that the tendencies in your own field differ considerably. We begin our discussion of citation verb tense and aspect with an analysis of the literature review of a published article.

Task Twenty-One

Read through this review of the literature on homelessness and happiness. Each of the citations has been bolded. The abstract is provided to give you an overall sense of the study. For each sentence that contains a citation or citations, identify as either a single study citation (SS) or a citation to a group of studies (GS) using the blanks on the right. Also indicate what verb form is used in the sentence with the citation: present tense (PresT), past tense (Past), or present perfect (PresPer). After characterizing each sentence with a citation, consider whether you see any pattern in terms of citation and tense, and then answer the questions after the text.

Social Indicators Research (2006) 76: 185–205

The Subjective Well-Being of the Homeless and Lessons for Happiness

Robert Biswas-Diener and Ed Diener

ABSTRACT. The current study assessed the subjective wellbeing of a broad spectrum of homeless people. One-hundred-and-eighty-six homeless people from the streets of Calcutta (India), California, and a tent camp in Portland (Oregon) were interviewed, and responded to measures of subjective well-being. They answered questions about life satisfaction, satisfaction with various life domains, and their experience of positive and negative emotions. The mean rating of life satisfaction was slightly negative for both American samples but positive for the pavement dwellers in Calcutta. Satisfaction with self-related domains was positive, whereas satisfaction with material related domains was generally negative. Satisfaction with social domains appears to be the area of largest variation among the groups. We discuss the importance of social factors and basic material needs as they relate to overall subjective well-being of the homeless.

KEY WORDS: homeless, quality of life, subjective well-being, well-being

Subjective Well-Being of the Homeless

(1) Poverty is one of the most pressing social concerns in the world today. (2) In 1999, according to the **United Nations Human Development Report (2002)**, nearly half the people in sub-Saharan Africa and more than a third of those in South East Asia lived on less than a dollar a day. (3) Of the poor, the most visible are the homeless. (4) Whether they are gangs of street youth or panhandling drifters, no society is unaffected by the social problem of homelessness. (5) There is little agreement about the possible causes and solutions to this social ill. (6) Although past research has focused on psychopathology, incidence of trauma, and the demography of the homeless, little attention has been paid in the psychological literature to the overall quality of life of the homeless. (7) Instead, the bulk of the research literature has been confined to clinical aspects of homelessness or to the effects of homelessness on children (**e.g., Aptekar, 1994**). (8) It is often assumed that life on the street is fraught with difficulty, but little information has been collected to suggest which specific life domains might be the least problematic, and in which areas, if any, the homeless might actually be flourishing. (9) Unfortunately, overlooking the possible resources and strengths of the homeless limits our ability to create effective interventions.

(10) The existing literature on homelessness strongly suggests that there are many problems associated with life without a home. (11) Studies have shown that homelessness is associated with problem behaviors in children (**Edleman and Mihaly, 1989; DiBiase and Waddell, 1995**), strained family relationships (**Vostanis et al., 1996; Nyamathi et al., 1999**), higher exposure to trauma (**Hien and Bukzpan, 1999; Buhrich et al., 2000**), increased anger and depression (**Marshall et al., 1996**), and the negative psychological impact of social stigma (**Lankenau, 1999**). (12) Because of the methodological difficulties related to studying homeless-

Study type
(SS or GS)
Verb Tense
and Aspect

ness, it is unclear whether factors such as depression and alcohol abuse are causes or effects of homelessness. ⑬ While prior history of mental illness is undoubtedly responsible for homelessness in at least some cases, there is evidence to suggest that the experience of homelessness causes or exacerbates many psychological problems. ⑭ In a study by **Shlay (1994)**, for example, homeless people were found to report greater emotional well-being and fewer behavioral problems in their children after positive changes in their economic and social status. ⑮ The need for research on personal resources and successes on the street becomes more pressing to the extent that people can overcome the psychological ills that accompany homelessness. ⑯ Studies on the harmful effects of homelessness are consistent with a larger body of literature examining the relation between income and subjective well-being. ⑰ In large national surveys, for example, income has been shown to be moderately correlated with life satisfaction, especially at the lower economic levels and in the poorest countries **(Diener et al., 1999; Diener & Lucas, 2000; Diener & Biswas-Diener, 2002)**. ⑱ Higher income has been shown to be related to increased longevity **(Wilkenson, 1996)**, better health **(Salovy et al., 2000)**, and greater life satisfaction **(Diener et al., 1985; Diener & Oishi, 2000)**. ⑲ Scholars appear to agree that although correlations between income and subjective well-being are often modest, there appears to be a curvilinear relationship in which money has the greatest impact on psychological health at the lowest economic levels **(Inglehart & Klingemann, 2000)**.

⑳ Two theories are often advanced to explain these findings: basic needs and adaptation. ㉑ In the former theory, it is assumed that basic physical needs such as food, water, and shelter, must be satisfied before a person can attain higher order psychological fulfillment **(Maslow, 1954)**. ㉒ By this reasoning, homeless individuals, who face impediments to fulfilling basic needs, should exhibit lower levels of subjective well-being. ㉓ As homeless people gain better access to food and shelter there ought to be a corresponding increase in psycho- logical health. ㉔ The theory of adaptation is also helpful in understanding the relation between income and subjective well-being. ㉕ Research on adaptation suggests that diminished responsiveness to repeated stimuli allows people to adjust to life circumstances, including adverse circumstances (**Silver, 1982; Loewenstein & Frederick, 1999**). ㉖ But while people can often adapt relatively well to discrete instances of trauma, there are conditions to which it is more difficult to adapt. ㉗ **Stroebe et al.** (**1996**), for instance, found that widows show higher average levels of depression than their non-bereaved counterparts, even 2 years after the death of their spouse. ㉘ A review of income and national happiness data by **Diener & Diener** (**1995**) showed lower levels of social well-being in poor nations, suggesting that extreme poverty is a condition difficult to adapt to, even in the long run.

Questions for Further Analysis

1. In the text on pages 49–51, do single studies or groups of studies tend to co-occur with present perfect? And which with past tense? What conclusions can you draw with regard to present perfect?

2. What kinds of citations (SS or GS) tend to co-occur with present tense?

3. In the text, what is interesting about the way Sentences 11 and 18 are written?

Tense choice in reviewing previous research is subtle and somewhat flexible. (It is also *not* much like the "rules" you may have been taught in English classes.) The following, therefore, are only general guidelines for tense usage.

Several studies have shown that at least two-thirds of all citing statements fall into one of these three major patterns.

I. Past—Reference to a Single Study (often an integral reference to researcher activity or findings)

Arslan (2007) *investigated* the performance characteristics of biodiesel as a diesel engine fuel.

The performance characteristics of biodiesel as a diesel engine fuel *were investigated* by Arslan (2007).

Biodiesel *was shown* to have promise as an alternative to regular diesel (Arslan, 2007).

II. Present Perfect—Reference to an Area of Inquiry (generally non-integral citations)

The potential of biodiesel as an alternative to regular diesel *has been* widely *investigated* (Savage, 2005; Pinnarat, 2006; Arslan, 2007).

There *have been* several investigations of the potential of biodiesel as an alternative to regular diesel (Savage, 2005; Pinnarat, 2006; Arslan, 2007).

Many researchers *have investigated* the potential of biodiesel as an alternative to regular diesel.[1–3]

III. Present—Reference to Generally Accepted Knowledge of the Field

The scarcity of known petroleum reserves is making renewable energy resources increasingly attractive (Savage, 2005; Pinnarat, 2006; Demirbas, 2007).

The scarcity of known petroleum reserves is making renewable energy resources increasingly attractive.[1–3]

All three patterns tend to occur in many extensive literature reviews because they add *variety* to the text.

Tense and aspect choices also tend to be associated with particular reporting verbs (see pages 54–55). For instance, verbs that have to do with arguments, claims, statements, and suggestions (e.g., *argue, suggest, claim,* or *maintain*) tend to be used in the present (Charles, 2006). Past tense is more likely to be chosen for verbs related with finding and showing (e.g., *find, identify, reveal,* or *indicate*) (Charles, 2006).

As we said earlier, these three patterns cover about two-thirds of the cases. The reason this proportion is not higher is because writers of literature reviews can have certain options in their choices of tenses. This is particularly true of Pattern I. The main verbs in Pattern I can refer to what a previous researcher *did* (*investigated, studied, analyzed,* etc.). By and large, in these cases the past is obligatory. However, the main verbs can also refer to what the previous researcher *wrote* or *thought* (*stated, concluded, claimed,* etc.). With this kind of reporting verb tense options are possible.

Pinnarat (2006) concluded that biodiesel production costs can be reduced by . . .

Pinnarat (2006) has concluded that . . .

Pinnarat (2006) concludes that . . .

Comparable options exist in the subordinate clause.

Evans et al. (2007) found that antibiotic resistance *was* increasing in U.S. hospitals.

Evans et al. (2007) have found that antibiotic resistance *is* increasing in U.S. hospitals.

Evans et al. (2007) found that antibiotic resistance *is* increasing in U.S. hospitals.

Evans et al. (2007) have found that antibiotic resistance *was* increasing in U.S. hospitals.

The differences among these tenses are subtle. In general, a move from past to present perfect and then to present indicates that the research reported is increasingly *close* to the writer in some way: close to the writer's own opinion, or close to the writer's own research, or close to the current state of knowledge.

This kind of present tense choice is sometimes called the *citational present* and is also used with famous or important sources.

Plato argues that . . .

Confucius says . . .

The Bible says . . .

The first sentence shows that the writer believes that the finding should be understood within the context of the single study. In the second and third, the writer implies that a wider generalization is possible.

Thus far, we have concentrated on the three main citation patterns. There are, of course, some others.

According to McCusker (2006), children and adolescents consuming caffeine in high concentrations suffered from caffeine-induced headaches.

As indicated by McCusker's (2006) research, children and adolescents consuming caffeine in high concentrations suffered from caffeine-induced headaches.

In the view of McCusker (2006), children and adolescents consuming caffeine in high concentrations suffered from caffeine-induced headaches.

McCusker's 2006 paper on caffeinated beverages concluded that children and adolescents consuming caffeine in high concentrations suffered from caffeine-induced headaches.

Can you think of any others?

Reporting Verbs

Good writers of literature reviews employ a range of patterns in order to vary their sentences. Good writers also employ a variety of reporting verbs in their literature reviews. A study by Ken Hyland (1999) identified more than 400 different reporting verbs; however, nearly 50 percent of these were used only one time in his corpus of 80 research articles. A much smaller number of verbs tend to predominate. Table 5 provides the most frequently used reporting verbs from a variety of disciplines, with the most frequent on the left and the sixth most frequent on the far right. As you can see, there are some disciplinary differences.

TABLE 5. High-Frequency Reporting Verbs

Discipline	Verbs and Frequency					
Rank	1	2	3	4	5	6
Harder Sciences						
Biology	describe	find	report	show	suggest	observe
Physics	develop	report	study	find	expand	
Electrical Engineering	propose	use	describe	show	publish	develop
Mechanical Engineering	describe	show	report	discuss	give	develop
Epidemiology	find	describe	suggest	report	examine	show
Nursing	find	suggest	report	identify	indicate	show
Medicine	show	report	demonstrate	observe	find	suggest
Softer Sciences						
Marketing	suggest	argue	find	demonstrate	propose	show
Applied Linguistics	suggest	argue	show	explain	find	point out
Psychology	find	show	suggest	report	demonstrate	focus
Sociology	argue	suggest	describe	note	analyze	discuss
Education	find	suggest	note	report	demonstrate	provide
Philosophy	say	suggest	argue	claim	point out	think

Source: Based on Swales, J.M., and C.B. Feak. (2004). *Academic Writing for Graduate Students: Essential Skills and Tasks*, 2d ed. Ann Arbor: University of Michigan Press.

It is important to point out that there are also differences in the frequency of reporting verb use among the different disciplines. For example, research papers in Physics have on average only about seven reporting verbs per paper, while in Philosophy, we find on average 57 per paper. In general, papers in the social sciences contain more reporting verbs than those in Engineering and other hard sciences.

Task Twenty-Two

Look again at Table 5, and consider these questions.

1. Are some verbs common to most fields? Which ones?

2. Compare the reporting verbs in Philosophy and Marketing. How similar are the two fields? What would account for this?

3. Now compare Philosophy and Medicine. How similar are the two fields? What would account for this?

4. Are there verbs that you would have expected to be in the table but are not among the top six? What are they?

5. Take a look at the reporting verbs in 3–4 articles or a literature review in a dissertation from your field. How well do the verb choices match with Hyland's findings and how well do they match with your own intuition?

Ambiguity in Citations

Citations, whether integral or non-integral, can sometimes be ambiguous or partly ambiguous as to whether the writer means to imply that somebody else *said/claimed/concluded* something or actually *did/found/carried out* something. Such citations have been called "hanging" citations by at least one editor in our field, who announced that he would no longer accept them. Even experienced research writers can run into problems here, whether they are using author-date references or number references. Ambiguity may be particularly difficult to avoid in number systems, especially if reference numbers are placed at the ends of sentences. Regardless, care should be taken so that your references are as clear as possible.

Task Twenty-Three

Consider the citations in this discussion of burnout and the related questions that follow.

① Researchers have been paying increasing attention to the concept of burnout, a work-related stress reaction that can be found among employees in a wide variety of occupations (Bakker, Demerouti, & Schaufeli, 2002). ② Most contemporary researchers agree that the syndrome is characterized by three related, but empirically distinct, elements: namely exhaustion, cynicism, and reduced professional efficacy (Leiter & Schaufeli, 1996; Maslach, Jackson, & Leiter, 1996; Maslach & Leiter, 1997). ③ Feelings of exhaustion or energy depletion are generally considered a core symptom of the burnout syndrome (Shirom, 1989). ④ Cynicism refers to the development of negative, cynical attitudes toward work and the people with whom one works (e.g., clients and colleagues). ⑤ The third dimension of burnout, reduced professional efficacy refers to the belief that one is no longer effective in fulfilling one's job responsibilities. ⑥ Thus, burned-out individuals suffer from feelings of fatigue, behave indifferently toward their work and clients, and they believe that their performance has suffered accordingly.

Source: Bakker, Arnold B., Hetty van Emmerik & Martin C. Euwema. 2006. Crossover of burnout and engagement in work teams. *Work and Occupation, 33*, 464–489.

1. How should the citation in Sentence 1 be read? Are Bakker, Demerouti, and Schaufeli (2002), major researchers in their fields, used to demonstrate the increasing interest? Are they the originators of the definition of *burnout* provided? Or are they perhaps commentators, with the citations referring to review or summary articles?

2. In Sentence 2, how are the three elements related to the citations? Are the three citations to be associated with all three of them or one element each? If one element should be associated with one citation, how should the placement of the citations be changed?

3. Sentence 3 is potentially ambiguous as well. Did Shirom draw this conclusion based on his/her reading of the literature or did he/she conclude this based on original research?

Because we cannot easily answer the questions surrounding the citations, they should probably be rewritten so that the intended meaning is conveyed. For instance, if the definition should be associated with Bakker, Demrouti, and Schaufeli, the information in Sentence 1 could be "repackaged" in this manner.

In recent years growing attention has been paid to the concept of burnout. Burnout has been defined as a work-related stress reaction that can be found among employees in a wide variety of occupations (Bakker, Demerouti, & Schaufeli, 2002).

Task Twenty-Four

Read the text and consider whether the citations are clear. The citations have been numbered and are superscripted. Can you determine whether the citations refer to research or to commentary, or are they ambiguous? Put an A in the space next to those that you think are ambiguous.

Almost all psychological research on humor has been associated with the assumption that positive personal characteristics might improve psychological well-being (1)(Kuiper et al., 2004). 1. _____
In addition, numerous studies have revealed that humor can improve psychological and physical well-being (2)(Lefcourt et al., 1990; Martin & Lefcourt, 1983; Porterfield, 1987), reduce 2. _____
the risk of cardiovascular disease (3)(Kerkkanen et al., 2004), 3. _____
and improve social relations (4)(Morreall, 1991). These findings have also indicated that humor can reduce occupational 4. _____
stress and that people with a good sense of humor also possess positive characteristics, such as being optimistic and having self-esteem and autonomy (5)(Martin et al., 1993; Overholser, 5. _____
1992). Furthermore, research has shown that people with a high sense of humor can overcome stress, usually experience fewer negative emotions, are physically healthy, and have good relations with others (6)(Martin, 1998; McGhee, 1982). 6. _____

(7)Abel, (2002) revealed that participants in a high sense of   7. _____
humor group were experiencing less stress and less current anx-
iety than those within a low sense of humor group, although
both groups had been coping with a similar number of everyday problems over a two month period.

Source: Tümkaya, S. (2007). Burnout and humor relationship among university lecturers. *Humor: International Journal of Humor Research 20,* 73–92.

Now try to rewrite one of the citations in the humor text so it no longer is
ambiguous.

Drafting, Redrafting, and Redrafting Again

In this section we introduce a case study of Joyce, who is a doctoral candidate in the post-secondary division of a well-known school of education. She is writing her dissertation on the role and function of the dissertation in U.S. education. She is still trying to come up with a title.

She has been busy on her literature review. So far, she has drafts of sections on the history of the dissertation in the United States, the role of graduate schools as "moderators," and how and why U.S. practices and perceptions may be somewhat different from those elsewhere. Being a diligent scholar, she has now discovered—to her great surprise—that a number of applied linguists have in recent years been examining the structures of dissertations (or PhD theses), typically for the purposes of helping students (especially international students) with this onerous task. Joyce has therefore decided to add a section covering this aspect of the literature. Her notes of what she has found are given in Task Twenty-Five.

Joyce learned from her reading that there are three types of dissertation (see page 61).

Figure 3. Three Types of Dissertation

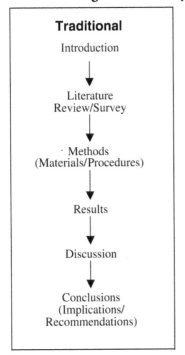

Traditional

Introduction

↓

Literature
Review/Survey

↓

· Methods
(Materials/Procedures)

↓

Results

↓

Discussion

↓

Conclusions
(Implications/
Recommendations)

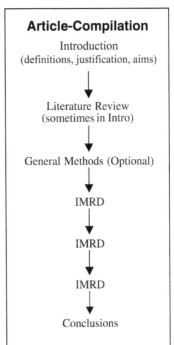

Article-Compilation

Introduction
(definitions, justification, aims)

↓

Literature Review
(sometimes in Intro)

↓

General Methods (Optional)

↓

IMRD

↓

IMRD

↓

IMRD

↓

Conclusions

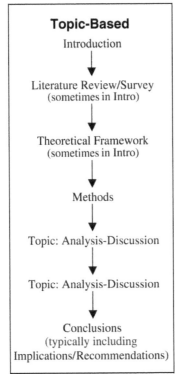

Topic-Based

Introduction

↓

Literature Review/Survey
(sometimes in Intro)

↓

Theoretical Framework
(sometimes in Intro)

↓

Methods

↓

Topic: Analysis-Discussion

↓

Topic: Analysis-Discussion

↓

Conclusions
(typically including
Implications/Recommendations)

Task Twenty-Five

Now read Joyce's summaries of her reading, and consider these questions.

1. Are all of the studies relevant?

2. How might you group them?

3. Which study (or studies) would you begin with?

A. **Dissertation Handbook, Rackham School of Graduate Studies (2005): The University of Michigan**

"You may submit as your dissertation a collection of closely related manuscripts based on research that you have conducted at the University of Michigan. The body of the dissertation may be composed of published and/or publication ready manuscripts, and the collection will have a coherent topic or theme. . . . Each manuscript may serve as a chapter and you may include a bibliography with each chapter or provide only one at the end of the dissertation" (p. 20).

B. **Dong (1998)**

She surveyed graduate students and faculty at U of Georgia and Georgia Institute of Technology in the science and engineering departments in the mid-1990s. Overall 38 percent of the students were using the article compilation format as opposed to the traditional IMRD one. The use of the article compilation format was significantly higher among native speakers than non-native speakers. Graduate students felt that the audience for the traditional dissertation was the advisor, committee, and colleagues working in the same lab; in the new anthology format, the audience broadened to a more general scientific community. Also advisors did more of the actual writing in the anthology format.

C. **Stålhammer (1998)**

She examined dissertations in social science departments at Gothenberg University in Sweden completed between 1984 and 1993 and found that the anthology format was more common in psychology than in other fields.

D. Bunton (1998)

Bunton analyzed 21 texts, 13 recent PhD theses and 8 M.Phil theses at the University of Hong Kong. Ten were from science and technology and 11 from humanities and social sciences. Only 3 of the texts followed the traditional pattern. Nine were basically article compilation, while the remaining 9 were "topic-based." These last were all from the social sciences and humanities; all used qualitative approaches and "report and discuss their analyses in multiple chapters (ranging from three to seven) with topic-specific titles" (p. 110).

E. Thompson (1999)

He examined 14 theses from the school of agriculture at University of Reading, United Kingdom. Only one was "traditional," 7 were article compilations with each of the chapters in IMRD format, while 6 were topic-based. The agricultural botanists preferred the anthology format, while the agricultural economists largely opted for the topic-based "componential format," applying the theoretical models they had developed to a series of case studies.

F. Paltridge (2002)

He examined 15 dissertations from a broad range of fields completed at an Australian university. His data are hard to interpret, but it looks as though six dissertations were traditional and five were article compilations and four were topic-based. Since he had only one or two examples from each field, it is probably risky to draw any disciplinary conclusions.

G. Swales (2004)

Swales surveyed recent dissertations from Mathematics, Physics, and Biology at the University of Michigan. All of the math ones were traditional, but the others were mostly article compilations. However, there were considerable internal variations. Of the eight Physics dissertations, five had a consolidated bibliography at the end, one included references at the end of each chapter, while two did both! In a few cases, the article nature was apparent from such phrases as "in this paper, we study . . . ," but most writers opted for formulations such as "in this chapter, I discuss." These latter he described as "hybrids."

First Draft

① It seems that six pieces of research have examined the structure of PhD theses or dissertations. ② Dong (1998) surveyed graduate students and faculty in science and engineering departments at two universities in the southeast of the United States, and found on average that 38 percent of the students were using the article compilation or "anthology" format. ③ In another study, Stålhammer (1998) found that the compilation format was common in the psychology department of a Swedish University. ④ Other research has been conducted in Hong Kong, Britain, and Australia. ⑤ Bunton (1998) in Hong Kong reports that nine of the 21 theses he examined were of the article compilation type, while only three used the traditional format. ⑥ The remaining three were "topic based" in that they contained several chapters, each dealing with a specific aspect or "topic" of the results. ⑦ This type was particularly common in qualitative studies in the humanities and social sciences. ⑧ Thompson (1999) focused on the structure of dissertations in a school of agriculture in southern England and reported similar findings. ⑨ Only one was traditional; seven were article compilation, while six were topic-based. Paltridge (2002) conducted a similar study in Australia, but with only one or two texts from each field; he found that the traditional dissertation was more common than in Thompson's data. ⑩ Finally, Swales (2004) examined dissertations at a research university in the United States; the mathematics dissertations were all traditional, while those in physics and biology were mostly article compilations. ⑪ It is worth noting that the latter option is accepted in the official dissertation handbook of this university.

1. How is the literature in this first draft organized?

2. How does Joyce introduce the literature? Does she use author-prominent (part of the sentence) or research-prominent (parenthetical) citations? What effect does this have on the flow of ideas?

3. What verbs does Joyce use to introduce the different studies? Is there enough variety?

4. In Sentence 1 Joyce begins with *It seems that* . . . . Do you think this was a good choice for the opening sentence? What does the word *seem* suggest to readers?

5. Joyce uses quite a few quotation marks or scare quotes. Why? What does this tell the readers?

6. There is quite a lot of information on the countries in which certain dissertation formats are common. How important is this information?

7. Has Joyce included any evaluation of the previous literature? In other words, do we have a sense of what she thinks about the quality and value of the work?

8. What do you think is the purpose of Sentence 11?

9. Based on the limited information here, can you think of some limitations in the existing research?

10. Does this review seem to point to Joyce's own possible contribution to this area of research? Is it important that she do so at this stage? (Sample answers for the tasks in this section on drafting and redrafting can be found in the *Commentary* at www.press.umich.edu/esl/compsite/ETRW/.)

Finally, the advisor told Joyce that the section of her literature was "flat and boring." In response to this comment, Joyce produced Draft 2. What would you expect to find in this second draft?

Second Draft

① There is, in fact, a small, growing and fascinating collection of recent studies that have examined the structure of the dissertation. ② Given their limited number, their geographical distribution is amazingly wide. ③ There are two studies from the United States (Dong, 1998; Swales, 2004) and single studies from Sweden (Stålhammer, 1998), Hong Kong (Bunton, 1998), the United Kingdom (Thompson, 1999), and Australia (Paltridge, 2002). ④ We thus have a global snapshot of what has been going on in recent years in terms of dissertation structure. ⑤ Overall, the findings indicate that the alternative anthology format is alive and well, especially in science, technology, and engineering.

⑥ According to Dong (1998), students like this new structure because it is closer to research reality, especially in terms of the fact that their audience is broadened from their examining committee to the research community at large. ⑦ Clearly, it is time for the traditional PhD dissertation to be given a decent burial.

Here are some of the advisor's reactions to this draft. Mark those that you think are reasonable (R) and those that are unreasonable (U).

_____ 1. "OK, Joyce, don't you think this is a bit overly enthusiastic? Do you really think the previous work is fascinating? And what's this about a global snapshot? Can you tone it down a bit?"

_____ 2. "I don't think it's your place to decide whether the traditional dissertation should be abandoned. I think you may be losing sight of your purpose."

_____ 3. "Do you think it really matters for your research work whether students like the new structure? You need to just focus on the different formats but not provide such extraneous evaluation."

_____ 4. "You haven't discussed any of the studies. You've grouped them together according to country, but is that the most meaningful way to approach these studies?"

_____ 5. "Try again."

Joyce then retreated to her computer, determined to demonstrate to her advisor that she could do much better.

Third Draft

① The previous section has shown that there is growing debate about the role and value of the doctoral dissertation as a "capstone" educational achievement. ② This in turn has led to a growing acceptance of alternatives to the traditional expanded IMRD format for the dissertation by many university authorities (such as *Dissertation Handbook*, University of Michigan, p. 20). ③ Perhaps because of these developments, a small, but widely distributed, body of research has recently emerged that attempts to investigate the *actual* structure of dissertations in a number of contexts. ④ According to these studies, the main departure from the "traditional" structure would seem to be that of an "article compilation," sometimes known as an "anthology" type (such as Dong, 1998). ⑤ Dong (1998) and Swales (2004) investigated the situation in the United States, the former finding that in the mid-1990s, 38 percent of the doctoral dissertations in science and engineering at two institutions had used this alternative format. ⑥ Swales' survey results from the University of Michigan suggest that—at least in this institution—article compilations were common in physics and biology, but not at all used in mathematics. ⑦ He also noted what he called "hybrids" in which articles prepared for publication took on the *appearance* of chapters in the dissertation itself.

⑧ Research elsewhere also points to innovative formats. Stålhammer (1998) investigated social science dissertations in Sweden and found that the anthology type was common in psychology, but less so in other departments. ⑨ However, recent studies from other countries (Bunton 1998 in Hong Kong; Thompson 1999 in the United Kingdom; and Paltridge 2002 in Australia) somewhat complicate the emerging picture. ⑩ One reason for this is that these three authors add a third category of dissertation, which is usually called "topic-based"; in this type, the results are broken up into several chapters, each with a topic-specific title. (11) In Hong Kong this last arrangement was especially preferred in the social sciences and the humanities; (12) in fact, only 3 of Bunton's 21 dissertations were traditional. (13) Thompson's (1999) research was more narrowly focused on a single school of agriculture in the United Kingdom, but even there he found that the agricultural botanists tended to opt for the anthology dissertation, while the agricultural economists selected a topic-based arrangement. (14) Finally, Paltridge (2002) examined 15 dissertations from several fields at an Australian university, identifying six as traditional, five as article compilations, and four topic-based. (15) Caution should be exercised when attempting to generalize from this data along with that of the other researchers, however, given the rather small sample number of dissertations examined. (16) While the overall data is indicative of possible trends and disciplinary differences, further work on this topic is necessary.

(17) Finally, it is worth noting that these studies have been conducted by discourse analysts and applied linguists, which perhaps has led to the primary focus on the structure of the texts themselves as opposed to the possible motivation for adopting one format or another. (18) Only Dong (1998) seriously considers the questions of how these alternative dissertation formats have emerged and what might be the possible *effects* of choosing one format over another, for both the advisor and the student. (19) It is this latter question, in particular that will be taken up in the next section, as I turn to the extensive literature on the mentoring relationships in doctoral programs.

1. How does this third draft strike you in terms of Joyce's positioning as a doctoral student/junior researcher? What do you think was the reaction of her advisor?

2. How is the information organized in this third draft? Does this make sense to you?

3. Has Joyce succeeded in striking a balance between description and evaluation? Are there any sections that are particularly well done?

4. How much do the comments at the end of the second paragraph and in the third paragraph contribute to Joyce's ability to conclude this section of her literature review?

5. Do you think Sentences 1 and 19 are useful? Why or why not?

6. Finally, what devices does Joyce use to maintain an overall good flow of ideas?

We hope that your answers allow you to see why Joyce's advisor was pleased with this third draft.

Taking a Stance toward the Literature

In Task Seven we focused on the possibility of using authors' perspectives toward the literature as one way to organize the discourse community literature. Using perspective as an organizing strategy may not be useful in your own literature review; however, perspective should play some role in the writing of your LR. Specifically, in many fields your reader(s) may expect to see in your LR your own perspective or stance toward the research of your field. This will require you to demonstrate not only what you know but also what you think about the work in your field.

Your stance[1] toward the literature can be revealed in a number of ways, some subtle and some obvious. You may recall this section from the LR on information overload. This excerpt includes some evaluation (in bold), indicating the author's take on the literature.

⑥ The **big** question with regard to effects of information overload is whether and how it impacts decision accuracy, decision time, and general performance. ⑦ While **research results have often been contradictory**, especially among the **groundbreaking studies** in marketing (the inconsistencies were in part due to methodological problems; see Jacoby et al., 1974; Malhotra et al., 1982; Muller, 1984), **there is wide consensus today** that heavy information load can affect the performance of an individual negatively (whether measured in terms of accuracy or speed).

The author characterizes the research in terms of inconsistencies and consensus (note the author's perspective that this consensus is broad), describing

---

[1] Your textual voice; your personal stamp of authority in relation to a text (Hyland, 2005).

certain work as groundbreaking. The use of *big* to describe the question also
. reveals the author's awareness of a central question in the field. This awareness could not be conveyed by the unmodified expression *one question.*

Looking again at the short text on homelessness and happiness from Task
Twenty-One, we again see that the authors do more than just report the literature. Note the use of *undoubtedly* in Sentence 13, which reveals the
authors' awareness that the information in the clause is likely already known
or is obvious (relating to or including readers in this manner can be referred
to as engaging the reader [Hyland, 2005]). Note how the authors exercise
caution in expressing their claims. In Sentence 13, they hedge the point
about mental illness by adding *in at least some cases.* They go on to say that
there is evidence to suggest, again revealing an awareness that the following
point must be softened. In Sentence 19, the authors cautiously say that
scholars appear to agree and again use *appear* later in that same sentence.

(12) Because of the methodological difficulties related to studying
homelessness, it is unclear whether factors such as depression and
alcohol abuse are causes or effects of homelessness. (13) While prior history of mental illness is undoubtedly responsible for homelessness in at
least some cases, there is evidence to suggest that the experience of
homelessness causes or exacerbates many psychological problems. . . .

(19) Scholars appear to agree that although correlations between
income and subjective well-being are often modest, there appears to
be a curvilinear relationship in which money has the greatest impact on
psychological health at the lowest economic levels (Inglehart &
Klingemann, 2000).

Finally, Joyce's third draft contains several expressions that reveal her stance toward the literature. Can you find them?

② This in turn has led to a growing acceptance of alternatives to the traditional expanded IMRD format for the dissertation by many university authorities (such as *Dissertation Handbook,* University of Michigan, p. 20). ③ Perhaps because of these developments, a small, but widely distributed, body of research has recently emerged that attempts to investigate the *actual* structure of dissertations in a number of contexts. ④ According to these studies, the main departure from the "traditional" structure would seem to be that of an "article compilation," sometimes known as an "anthology" type (such as Dong, 1998).

To perhaps better see how evaluative language and hedging contributes to author stance, look at this reformulation of Sentence 3, which lacks the evaluation of the original.

③ Because of these developments, a body of research has emerged to investigate the *actual* structure of dissertations in a number of contexts.

In his 2005 article, Hyland proposes that stance can be revealed through the use of these elements: hedges, boosters (words that strengthen a claim), attitude markers (words that indicate your attitude), and personal pronouns (such as *I* or *we*). Examples of the use of personal pronouns can be found in the section of Betty's LR highlighted in Task Thirteen, as well as the LR excerpt in Task Fourteen.

Task Twenty-Six

Revise the claims to reflect a perspective, using the information in italics. Try not to use any of the language in the italics. An example is provided.

Original

Email is a powerful communication tool for marketers. The efficacy of this tool is being eroded by the proliferation of spam.

You are disappointed that the effectiveness of email is quickly changing for the negative.

Revision

Email is a powerful communication tool for marketers. Unfortunately, the efficacy of this tool is rapidly being eroded by the proliferation of spam.

1. One behavioral finding is that indecisive individuals delay decision-making for a longer time than do decisive ones.

   You think the finding is very important.

   _____

   _____

2. The nature of natural warning signs of tsunamis poses challenges to providing useful information to the public. Furthermore, information about these signs makes public education difficult and recommending specific behavioral responses problematic.

   You think there is a wide variety of natural warning signs; you think the challenge is very important; you think the information about these signs differs greatly and there is no agreement.

   _____

   _____

   _____

3. Some traditional Chinese Medicine (TCM) treatments have become accepted by doctors in the U.S. and in Europe. TCM presents a completely new frame of reference for treating disease.

You think that there is rather broad acceptance among doctors and that these doctors are not on the fringe, but typical doctors.

_____

_____

_____

4. Mobile phones have come to infiltrate contemporary life. Such integrations of public and private space have left many of us questioning and reevaluating social norms and boundaries (Ling, 1997). For example, Ling found that 60 percent of mobile phone users, versus 76 percent of nonusers agreed or "tended to agree" with the statement that "the mobile phone disturbs other people" (Ling, 2004, p. 123). There is a disparity plaguing these two parties and an aching for an understanding of just how "intrusive" mobile telephones have become, and, how intrusive we should allow them to be.

You think that phones have infiltrated just about every part of life; you think the disparity between the two parties is quite obvious; you think your second point about how intrusive people should allow phones to be is more relevant than your first point about how intrusive they actually are.

_____

_____

_____

_____

_____

_____

Constructing an Original Discussion of Previous Work: Using Your Own Words

In this volume, we have essentially adopted a top-down approach to LR writing. As a result of this, we have not yet discussed one important challenge in writing the literature review, namely how to create your own original research story using your own words. In your LR you will likely be engaged in both paraphrasing and summarizing, which require you to restate—in your own words—information from other texts. The difference between the two is that a paraphrase is a restatement of a specific point or points from another work, while a summary focuses less on individual points and more on the main message of the source. Regardless of which you are doing, finding your own words can be difficult for a number of reasons. First, your text may be highly technical, thus limiting your options for using your own words, as in the first example given. Alternatively, synonyms or other grammatical variation may not be available, as demonstrated by the second example.

Consider:

Mouse monoclonal antibodies were produced against recombinant Sp17 protein and used in Western blot and immunohistochemical analyses of normal reproductive tissue and primary ovarian tumor samples.

The highly technical nature of this sentence will greatly limit any attempt at rewriting. No suitable alternatives are available for *mouse monoclonal antibodies, produced against, recombinant Sp17 protein, Western blot, immunohistochemical, normal reproductive tissue*, and *primary ovarian tumor samples*—just about the entire sentence.

Ankara is the capital of Turkey.

Can this really be stated in any other way apart from reversing the order of the information? *The capital of Turkey is Ankara.*

Second, it may seem that the source is so nicely written that any attempt to put it in your words will be unsuccessful.

It has not escaped our notice that the specific pairing we have postulated immediately suggests a possible copying mechanism for the genetic material (Crick & Watson, 1953).

You may recognize this as the legendary understatement at the end of the letter to *Nature* in which Crick and Watson reported on the double-helical structure of DNA. Note the strategic use of *immediately*, which Gross, a professor of rhetoric, argues instructs the reader from this point on to consider the DNA structure in an entirely new way (Gross, 1990).

Third, it is possible that you do not fully understand your source. This excerpt seems rather challenging to us and could be very difficult to restate.

Complexification simplifies behavior because the new, steep gradient forces energy to flow always in one direction. With the large flux on the gradient, positive feedbacks emerge until negative feedbacks generate constraints. When constraints are encountered inside the system, the behavior of the system's parts is reliably pinned against those constraints by the powerful flux down the gradient, making the system behave simply and predictably (Allen et al., 2001).

Fourth, you may have gaps in your vocabulary that prevent you from finding alternative ways of stating information from your source.

Although it may be difficult to find your own words, we suggest you work toward that goal so that you can reveal your understanding and create a text with a consistent writing style, neither of which can be achieved by stringing together a series of quotes or reusing strings of language from different sources (Flowerdew, 2007). (Note: Advisors can often detect borrowing and reuse of language because of a shift in style.) In addition, if you can use your own words you can avoid the issue of plagiarism.

Plagiarism is best defined as a deliberate activity—as the conscious copying from the work of others. The concept of plagiarism has become an integral part of scholarship and study in North American and Western European countries. It is based on a number of assumptions that may not hold true in all cultures. One is a rather romantic assumption that the writer is an original, individual, creative artist. Another is that original ideas and expressions are the acknowledged property of their creators (as is the case with a patent for an invention). Yet another is that it is a sign of disrespect—rather than respect—to copy without acknowledgment from the works of published authorities.

Of course, borrowing the words and phrases of others can be a useful language learning strategy. Certainly you would not be plagiarizing if you borrowed items that are commonly or frequently used in academic English or that are part of common knowledge.

Tashkent is the capital of Uzbekistan.

For every action there is an equal and opposite reaction.

The results from this experiment indicate that . . .

These results are statistically significant.

But do not borrow "famous" phrases without at least putting them in quotation marks. Here, for example is a famous quotation by physicist Edward Teller.

The science of today is the technology of tomorrow.

So, if you wanted to use the sentence, you should recognize its special status and place it in quotation marks.

You also need to be cautious about borrowing more than what may be considered standard phraseology—that is, borrowing content and ideas, not just commonly used expressions of academia in general and your field in particular. We would encourage you to borrow standard phraseology of your field and skeletal phrases when appropriate but not special expressions or long strings of language containing information specific to a particular publication.

Distinguishing between what is and what is not standard phraseology can be challenging, but if you have read widely during your course of study, you are likely aware of much of the language commonly used in academic writing. For instance, if we look again at the text on happiness and homelessness, you might have noticed some expressions that are frequently used. Those that you could likely use in your own writing have been bolded.

⑩ **The existing literature on** homelessness **strongly suggests that there are many problems associated with** life without a home. ⑪ **Studies have shown that** homelessness **is associated with** problem behaviors in children (Edleman & Mihaly, 1989; DiBiase & Waddell, 1995), strained family relationships (Vostanis et al., 1996; Nyamathi et al., 1999), higher exposure to trauma (Hien & Bukzpan, 1999; Buhrich et al., 2000), increased anger and depression (Marshall et al., 1996), and the negative psychological impact of social stigma (Lankenau, 1999). ⑫ **Because of the methodological difficulties related to studying** homelessness, **it is unclear whether** factors such as depression and alcohol abuse are causes or effects of homelessness. ⑬ While prior history of mental illness is undoubtedly responsible for homelessness in at least some cases, **there is evidence to suggest that** the experience of homelessness causes or exacerbates many psychological problems. ⑭ In a study by Shlay (1994), for example, homeless people were found to report greater emotional well-being and fewer behavioral problems in their children after positive changes in their economic and social status. ⑮ **The need for research on** personal resources and successes on the street becomes more pressing to the extent that people can overcome the psychological ills that accompany homelessness. ⑯ **Studies on** the harmful effects of homelessness **are consistent with a larger body of literature** examining the relation between income and subjective well-being. ⑰ In large national surveys, for example, income **has been shown to be moderately correlated with** life satisfaction, especially at the lower economic levels and in the poorest countries (Diener et al., 1999; Diener & Lucas, 2000; Diener & Biswas-Diener, 2002). (18) Higher income **has been shown to be related to** increased longevity (Wilkenson, 1996), better health (Salovy et al., 2000), and greater life satisfaction (Diener et al., 1985; Diener & Oishi, 2000). (19) **Scholars appear to agree that** although correlations between income and subjective well-being are often modest, there appears to be a curvilinear relationship in which money has the greatest impact on psychological health at the lowest economic levels (Inglehart & Klingemann, 2000).

Task Twenty-Seven

Here are some approaches to writing, beginning with a plagiarizing approach and ending with an acceptable quoting technique. Where does plagiarism stop? Draw a line between the last approach that would produce plagiarism and the first approach that would produce acceptable original work. (Sample answers for the tasks in this section on using your own words can be found in the *Commentary* available at www.press.umich.edu/esl/compsite/ETRW/.)

1. Copying a paragraph as it is from the source without any acknowledgment.

2. Copying a paragraph making only small changes, such as replacing a few verbs or adjectives with synonyms.

3. Cutting and pasting a paragraph by using the sentences of the original but leaving one or two out, or by putting one or two sentences in a different order.

4. Composing a paragraph by taking short standard phrases from a number of sources and putting them together with some words of your own.

5. Paraphrasing a paragraph by rewriting with substantial changes in language and organization, amount of detail, and examples.

6. Quoting a paragraph by placing it in block format with the source cited.

There is disagreement as to where to draw the line. Some draw the line after the third statement. Others are more inclined to draw it after the fourth. Clearly, statement three is a gray area. The degree to which a person follows the fourth approach is very important because care must be taken not to borrow too much. To be successful, you need to be able to identify standard phraseology, which can be borrowed, and the expressions chosen to uniquely express an idea.

To understand other perspectives on this issue, we recommend that you read through your university's plagiarism policy and discuss with your advisor or supervisor what kind of language borrowing would be acceptable. For example, where does your advisor stand on the question of copying, with only minimal changes, a standard methodology in your field?

Some Strategies for Paraphrasing

Let's say that you are writing your LR on driver aid systems (such as antilock brakes) that increase vehicle safety. You are working on a section describing the conditions under which accidents commonly occur. You find this interesting bit of information and want to include it.

> Contrary to the common belief that spinning of cars mainly occurs on slippery roads and at high speeds, the statistics show that by far most severe accidents occur on dry roads and at speeds between 60 km/h and 100 km/h (van Zanten, 2002).

You have two options for using the excerpt: quoting exactly as is or putting it into your own words. Given that the vocabulary is not highly technical and the point does not seem to be so eloquently written that you should worry about "ruining" it, we think the right choice is to use your own words. Also, recall that Hyland's study referred to in Task Nineteen found that no direct quotations were used in the papers published in the sciences. (Charles [2006] also found that direct quotes are not generally used in Materials Science dissertations.) So, let's work through some possible strategies to put this in your own words.

First determine the relevant points and the relationships among them.

Important points:

- the common belief is that spinning of cars mainly occurs on slippery roads and at high speeds
- most severe accidents occur on dry roads and at speeds between 60 km/h and 100 km/h

Relationships between the two points:

- common belief and fact are not in agreement

Linking phrases and expressions that can connect the two points:

- *although*
- *however*
- *while*
- *rather than*

Verbs that might establish other relationships:

- *due to*
- *caused by*
- *can be attributed to*

Next, consider the following possible synonyms for the source vocabulary and changing the part of speech (nouns to verbs, for instance):

- *spinning of cars → crashes?*
- *slippery → slick? wet?*
- *severe → serious? severity?*
- *dry → good conditions?*
- *occur → happen? take place? occurrence?*
- *most → the majority of?*
- *common → widespread?*
- *belief → believe? think?*

Additions or deletions:

- *include who holds the belief → people?*
- *include researchers?*
- *delete point about common belief?*

Task Twenty-Eight

Rewrite the idea from van Zanten using *however* and *as opposed to,* changing the vocabulary and grammar as necessary. Here is an example using the subordinator *although.*

<u>Example:</u> Begin with *although*

Although many people think that car accidents are more likely due to slick roads and high speeds, research shows that the majority of serious accidents occur on dry roads and at speeds of 60 to 100 km/h (van Zanten, 2002).

Although it is widely believed that most car accidents can be attributed to high speeds and poor road conditions, in fact, according to van Zanten, the majority of serious accidents occur when roads are dry and the vehicle is traveling between 60 and 100km/h (2002).

1. Use *however*

_____

_____

_____

_____

2. Use *as opposed to*

_____

_____

_____

_____

3. Write two paraphrases of this short text. Before writing, break the task into different parts as we did for the van Zanten excerpt.

> Ever increasing traffic forces the driver to process a growing amount of information and, at the same time, to take more, and quicker, decisions. Thus, in critical situations, the amount of information may exceed the driver's effective processing capability.

Important points:

Relationship between the points:

Linking phrases or expressions to connect the points:

Possible synonyms:

Paraphrase 1

_____

_____

_____

_____

Paraphrase 2

_____

_____

_____

Careful Use of Synonyms

When using synonyms, it is important to be careful about your choices. Not all synonyms work equally well in all contexts. Consider this example, for instance:

The public perception of vehicle systems and the benefits they offer are vital.

If you follow a simple synonym substitution process, you may produce something like this:

It is very important to consider the municipal views regarding vehicle systems and the advantages they give.

The rearrangement of the ideas is good and is an important strategy for paraphrasing. However, *public* and *municipal* are not quite similar enough. Perhaps *consumers* would be a better choice here. In addition, *advantages they give* does not work so well because the collocation—simply put, words that tend to go together—is awkward. *Provide* would be a better choice.

If you need to check whether a word works in a particular expression, check for it on the Internet, ideally Google Scholar. In your search place the expression in quotation marks and, if you think it would be helpful, place a wild card (*) in the expression so that you can capture variations of the expression. For instance, we searched for the following on Google Scholar. (Note: To narrow hits to your field of study also include a relevant term outside the quotation marks.)

"give * advantages" (approximately 4,300 hits)

"provide * advantages" (approximately 191,000 hits)

Given the approximately 191,000 hits for *provide*, this seems to be a better choice. So, a better restatement of the point may be this.

It is very important to consider consumer views regarding vehicle systems and the advantages they provide.

Summarizing

There are no guidelines to help you decide when you should summarize a portion of published work. However, if there is a previous study that warrants a more-detailed discussion, then you will most likely be summarizing the key aspects of that study that have a bearing on your own work.

Let's assume you are conducting research on ways to help blind people find their way to a given destination. You have been reviewing the previous work on this topic and discovered a paper by James Coughlan and Roberto Manduchi, which describes a wayfinding system based on cell phone technology. You have also been investigating the use of commercially available technology such as cell phones to guide blind people. Thus, this paper provides some very important background for your own work. In your literature review, you want to describe the system developed by Coughlan and Manduchi and presented in a paper entitled "Color Targets: Fiducials to

Help Visually Impaired People Find Their Way by Camera Phone." Here is the excerpt that you wish to summarize.

We propose a new assistive technology system to aid in wayfinding based on a camera cell phone (see Figure 1), which is held by the user to find and read aloud specially designed signs in the environment. These signs consist of barcodes placed adjacent to special landmark symbols. The symbols are designed to be easily detected and located by a computer vision algorithm running on the cell phone; their function is to point to the barcode to make it easy to find without having to segment it from the entire image. Our proposed system, which we have already prototyped, has the advantage of using standard off-the-shelf cell phone technology—which is inexpensive, portable, multipurpose, and becoming nearly ubiquitous—and simple color signs which can be easily produced on a standard color printer. Another advantage of the cell phone is that it is a mainstream consumer product which raises none of the cosmetic concerns that might arise with other assistive technology requiring custom hardware. Our system is designed to operate efficiently with *current* cell phone technology using machine-readable signs. Our main technological innovation is the design of special landmark symbols (i.e., fiducials), which we call *color targets*, that can be robustly detected and located in fractions of a second on the cell phone CPU, which is considerably slower than a typical desktop CPU. The color targets allow the system to quickly detect and read a linear barcode placed adjacent to the symbol. It is important that these symbols be detectable at distances up to several meters in cluttered environments, since a blind or visually impaired person cannot easily find a barcode in order to get close enough to it to be read. Once the system detects a color target, it guides the user towards the sign by providing appropriate audio feedback.

Source: *EURASIP Journal on Image and Video Processing* 2007, article ID 96357

Task Twenty-Nine

Read through this draft summary of Coughlan and Manduchi's system and then read the comments from an advisor that follow. Consider whether the comments are reasonable (R) or unreasonable (U) as well as how or whether to address them in a revision.

Draft Summary

Several authors have described the use of commercially available technology to assist blind people. For example, Coughlan and Manduchi describe a new system to assist in finding one's way based on a camera cell phone. In this system a cell phone is held by the user to find specially designed signs in the environment. These signs are made of barcodes placed next to special landmark symbols. The symbols are easily detected and located by a computer vision algorithm running on the cell phone; the symbols point to the barcode to make it easy to find without having to segment it from the entire image. Their system has the advantage of using standard off-the-shelf cell phone technology, which is affordable, portable, and widely available in stores. Another advantage is that the color signs are simple and easily produced on a standard color printer. Another advantage of the cell phone is that it is a consumer product that does not look like assistive technology requiring custom hardware. Their system operates efficiently with *current* cell phone technology using machine-readable signs. Their main technological innovation is the design of special landmark symbols (i.e., fiducials), which they call *color targets*. These targets can be strongly detected and located in fractions of a second on the cell phone CPU. The color targets allow the system to quickly detect and read a linear barcode placed adjacent to the symbol. In their system these symbols are detectable at distances up to several meters in cluttered environments, since a blind or visually impaired person cannot easily find a barcode in order to get close enough to it to be read. Once the cell phone system detects a color target, the user is guided towards the sign by providing appropriate audio feedback.

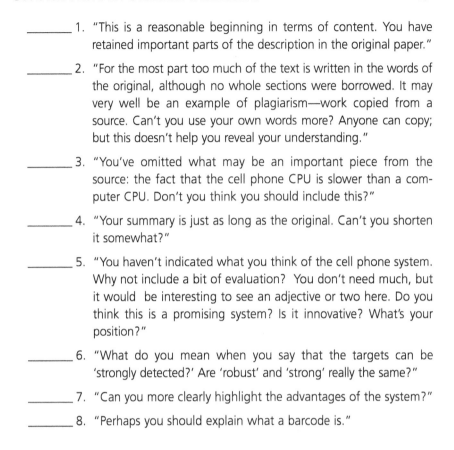

_____ 1. "This is a reasonable beginning in terms of content. You have retained important parts of the description in the original paper."

_____ 2. "For the most part too much of the text is written in the words of the original, although no whole sections were borrowed. It may very well be an example of plagiarism—work copied from a source. Can't you use your own words more? Anyone can copy; but this doesn't help you reveal your understanding."

_____ 3. "You've omitted what may be an important piece from the source: the fact that the cell phone CPU is slower than a computer CPU. Don't you think you should include this?"

_____ 4. "Your summary is just as long as the original. Can't you shorten it somewhat?"

_____ 5. "You haven't indicated what you think of the cell phone system. Why not include a bit of evaluation? You don't need much, but it would be interesting to see an adjective or two here. Do you think this is a promising system? Is it innovative? What's your position?"

_____ 6. "What do you mean when you say that the targets can be 'strongly detected?' Are 'robust' and 'strong' really the same?"

_____ 7. "Can you more clearly highlight the advantages of the system?"

_____ 8. "Perhaps you should explain what a barcode is."

Overall, although the summary is a reasonable draft, it is too close to the original to be used in its present form in an LR. Now, let us consider how this summary could be improved. You could try paraphrasing each sentence following the process outlined on pages 82–83. This, however, may not be enough to satisfy the advisor's need to see what you think. Perhaps a better strategy is to begin by identifying the points you need to support the claim that commercially available technology has been used to assist the blind in wayfinding and that this work is important.

Consider what information might be useful. The questions given here might help you identify what parts of the excerpt to include. Using the Coughlan and Manduchi text, answer the questions in your own words as much as possible, keeping in mind that technical vocabulary (such as _camera, computer,_ and _algorithm_) cannot be changed.

Question	Answer
What was done?	
How does it work?	
How was it done?	
Who did it?	
What is different/innovative/ advantageous?	

Note: You can devise your own questions when you summarize parts of papers from your own field. We thought the questions would be useful for the particular text on wayfinding technology and can help you find your own words.

In answering the questions, you may have extracted this information.

• A cell phone camera was used to assist blind people to find their way.

• The cell phone camera is used to find targets on paper signs printed on a typical computer printer; the signs have barcodes that are detected by the camera; the barcodes are transformed by an algorithm into an audio signal that indicates the direction to go.

• A computer algorithm was loaded onto a cell phone so that the barcodes can be transformed into audio directions for the user; the algorithm was presented in a previous paper by the authors.

• Coughlan and Manduchi did the work.

• The system is cheap; it's based on a regular cell phone and technology that is already available; it does not call attention to the user because cell phones are so widely used; it's fast.

• The design of special landmark symbols or *color targets* is a significant contribution.

How might this information be put together in a summary? This next task offers one possibility.

Task Thirty

Here is a second draft of the summary. Read and work through the questions that follow.

Several authors have described the use of commercially available technology to assist blind people. For example, recent innovative work by Coughlan and Manduchi involves the use of a cell phone camera and barcodes (similar to those found on store packaging) printed on paper to help blind people find their way. Wayfinding is accomplished in the following manner. The user holds the cell phone with the camera facing the desired direction of movement. When the camera detects a symbol or colored target, which the authors refer to as signs, the barcode is read and transformed via computer vision algorithm (previously developed by the authors) into audio feedback. This audio output then guides the user in the appropriate direction. The introduction of the colored targets, which can be easily created using a standard printer, offers the potential for improved guidance for the visually impaired that can be implemented with minimal cost.

This cell phone guidance system has four important advantages. First, it is inexpensive. Second, it is based on currently available technology rather than technology that is not available. Third, the system does not draw attention to the user, unlike other assistive devices, and can be discreetly used. Finally, the system is sufficiently fast so as to allow the user to efficiently reach the desired destination.

1. Does the summary capture the relevant information of the source?

2. To what extent has the author of the draft used his/her own words?

3. How well has the draft author revealed his/her understanding of the system?

4. Can you identify any instances of evaluation? Are these appropriate?

5. Try to write your own summary of the source text.

Because many of the summaries you write will be woven into your own original text, it may be very important to identify at least the source author, depending on your field of study. Refer back to the earlier discussion on citation patterns (pages 43–59) for some ideas.

Note that references to authors nearly always includes the family names only. First names are not used in in-text citations because this makes it difficult for your reader to know to whom you might be referring.

In a longer summary, you may want to remind your reader that you are summarizing.

The author goes on to say that . . .

The article further states that . . .

(author's family name here) also states/maintains/argues that . . .

(author's family name here) also believes that . . .

(author's family name here) concludes that . . .

In the second half of the paper, (author's surname here) presents . . .

In fact, if your summary is quite long you may want to mention the source author's name at different points in your summary—the beginning, the middle, and/or the end. When you do mention the author in the middle or end of the summary, be sure to use the family name only. Here are some examples.

The model proposed by Goodman further explains why . . .

Bradley et al. also found that . . .

The author further argues that . . .

Some of these sentence connectors may be useful in introducing additional information.

| additionally | in addition to | furthermore |
| also | further | |

Criteria for Evaluating
Literature Reviews

As we reported earlier, Boote and Beile (2005) argue that doctoral students should first be scholars before researchers. In other words, researchers should demonstrate a fairly comprehensive understanding of the previous work in their field before undertaking research. They argue that if students have a depth of understanding of past work this will lead to greater methodological sophistication in their own research. While Boote and Beile's focus is on education, the framework they provide for evaluating that understanding as revealed in an LR may be useful in many disciplines.

Although your advisors will have specific expectations for your LR, we offer here the general criteria from Boote and Beile (2005) for you to consider as you evaluate your own work.

Task Thirty-One

Look over the rubric in Table 6 and consider which of the criteria would be most important for a thesis or dissertation LR in your fields. Which of the criteria might be relevant for a journal article?

TABLE 6. A Possible LR Scoring Rubric

Category	Criterion	1	2	3	4
1. Coverage	A. Justified criteria for inclusion and exclusion from review.	Did not discuss the criteria inclusion or exclusion	Discussed the literature included and excluded	Justified inclusion and exclusion of literature	
2. Synthesis	B. Distinguished what has been done in the field from what needs to be done.	Did not distinguish what has and has not been done	Discussed what has and has not been done	Critically examined the state of the field	
	C. Placed the topic or problem in the broader scholarly literature.	Topic not placed in broader scholarly literature	Some discussion of broader scholarly literature	Topic clearly situated in broader scholarly literature	
	D. Placed the research in the historical context of the field.	History of topic not discussed	Some mention of history of topic	Critically examined history of topic	
	E. Acquired and enhanced the subject vocabulary.	Key vocabulary not discussed	Key vocabulary defined	Discussed and resolved ambiguities in definitions	
	F. Articulated important variables and phenomena relevant to the topic.	Key variables and phenomena not discussed	Reviewed relationships among key variables and phenomena	Noted ambiguities in literature and proposed new relationships	
	G. Synthesized and gained a new perspective on the literature.	Accepted literature at face value	Some critique of literature	Offered new perspective	
3. Methodology	H. Identified the main methodologies and research techniques that have been used in the field, and their advantages and disadvantages.	Research methods not discussed	Some discussion of research methods used to produce claims	Critiqued research methods	Introduced new methods to address problems with predominant methods
	I. Related ideas and theories in the field to research methodologies.	Research methods not discussed	Some discussion of appropriateness of research methods to warrant claims	Critiqued appropriateness of research methods to warrant claims	
4. Significance	J. Rationalized the practical significance of the research problem.	Practical significance of research not discussed	Practical significance discussed	Critiqued practical significance of research	
	K. Rationalized the scholarly significance of the research problem.	Scholarly significance of research not discussed	Scholarly significance discussed	Critiqued scholarly significance of research	
5. Rhetoric	L. Was written with a coherent, clear structure that supported the review.	Poorly conceptualized, haphazard	Some coherent structure	Well developed, coherent	

Note: The column-head numbers represent scores for rating dissertation literature reviews on 3-point and 4-point scales. Used with permission by Sage (from Boote & Beile, borrowed from Hart 2005).

Some Final Thoughts to Consider

As we come to the end of *Telling a Research Story*, we need to return to the "big picture." So, as a closing activity we ask you to relate your LR to these points.

Answer each of these as yes (Y), no (N), or unsure (U) in regard to your own LR.

_____ 1. Have you shaped your LR to fit your research questions or hypotheses?

_____ 2. Have you appropriately grouped your various sources?

_____ 3. Have you struck an appropriate balance between description and evaluation?

_____ 4. If your LR is lengthy or complex, have you used a sufficient amount of metadiscourse to guide your readers and ensure they can see the research story that is unfolding?

_____ 5. Have you sufficiently explained why certain sources were included or excluded?

_____ 6. If appropriate for your field, have you included both author prominent (integral) and research prominent (non-integral) citations?

_____ 7. Have you used a variety of reporting verbs and structures?

_____ 8. Have you chosen the right verb tenses for your citations?

_____ 9. Are there possibly any "missing inputs" that your readers or reviewers are likely to pick up on? In other words have you adequately covered the research territory?

_____ 10. Have you described the literature in an original manner so that questions of plagiarism will not arise?

References

Bakker, A. B., van Emmerick, H., & Euwema, M. C. (2006). Crossover of burnout and engagement of teams. *Work and Occupation, 33*, 464–489.

Bavelas, J. (1978). The social psychology of citations. *Canadian Psychological Review 19*, 158–163.

Biswas-Diener, R., & Diener, E. (2006). The subjective well-being of the homeless and lessons for happiness. *Social Indicators Research, 76*, 185–205.

Boote, D., & Beile, P. (2005). Scholars before researchers: On the centrality of the dissertation literature review in research preparation. *Educational Researcher, 34*(6), 3–15.

Budin, W. (2002, Summer). Beyond books and journals: Electronic and web based resources to facilitate research. *The Research Connection, 5–6.*

Charles, M. (2006). Phraseological patterns in reporting clauses used in citation: A corpus-based study of theses in two disciplines. *English for Specific Purposes, 25*(3), 310–331.

Crismore, A., & Farnsworth, R. (1990). Metadiscourse in popular and professional science discourse. In Walter Nash (Ed.), *The writing scholar: Studies in academic discourse* (pp. 118–136). Newbury Park, CA: Sage.

Eppler, J. M., & Menghis, J. (2006). The concept of information overload: A review of the literature from organization science, accounting, marketing, MIS, and related disciplines. *The Information Society, 20,* 323–344.

Flowerdew, J. (2007). The non-Anglophone scholar on the periphery of scholarly publication. *AILA Review, 20*(1), 14–27.

Gilbert, G. N. (1977). Referencing as persuasion. *Social Studies of Science, 7,* 113–122.

Hart, C. (2005). *Doing a literature review: Releasing the social science.* London: Sage.

Hyland, K. (1998). Persuasion and context: The pragmatics of academic metadiscourse. *Journal of Pragmatics, 30*(4), 437–455.

———. (1999). Academic attribution: Citation and the construction of disciplinary knowledge. *Applied Linguistics, 20*(3), 341–367.

————. (2005). Stance and engagement: A model of interaction in academic discourse. *Discourse Studies, 7*(2), 173–191.

Mauranen, A. (1993). *Cultural differences in academic rhetoric: A textlinguistic study.* Frankfurt: Peter Lang.

Maxwell, J. A. (2006). Literature reviews of, and for, educational research: A commentary on Boote and Beile's "Scholars Before Researchers." *Educational Researcher, 35*(9), 28–31.

Myers, G. (1991). Stories and styles in two molecular biology review articles. In C. Bazerman & J. Paradis (Eds.), *Textual dynamics of the professions* (pp. 45–75). Madison: University of Wisconsin Press.

Noguchi, J. (2006). *The science review article: An opportune genre in the construction of science.* Berlin: Peter Lang.

Paltridge, B., & Starfield, S. (2007). *Thesis and dissertation writing in a second language: A handbook for supervisors.* London: Routledge.

Ravetz, J. R. (1971). *Scientific knowledge and its social problems.* Oxford: Clarendon Press.

Samraj, B. (1995). *The nature of academic writing in an interdisciplinary field.* Unpublished doctoral dissertation, University of Michigan, Ann Arbor.

Singer P., Pellegrino, E., & Siegler, M. (2001). Clinical ethics revisited. *BMC Medical Ethics, 2,* 1.

Swales, J. M. (1990). *Genre analysis.* Cambridge, UK: Cambridge University Press.

Swales, J. M., & Feak, C. B. (2004). *Academic writing for graduate students: Essential skills and tasks* (2nd ed.). Ann Arbor: University of Michigan Press.

Tümkaya, S. (2007). Burnout and humor relationship among university lecturers. *Humor: International Journal of Humor Research, 20,* 73–92.

Torraco, R. J. (2005). Writing integrative literature reviews: Guidelines and examples. *Human Resource Development Review, 4*(3), 356–367.

White, H. D. (2001). Authors as citers over time. *Journal of American Society for Information Science, 52,* 87–108.

Williams, J. M. (2007). *Style: Ten lessons in clarity and grace.* New York: Pearson Longman.